Learning Later

Learning Later

Fresh Horizons in English Adult Education

Enid and Edward Hutchinson

ROUTLEDGE & KEGAN PAUL
London, Henley and Boston

First published in 1978
by Routledge & Kegan Paul Ltd
39 Store Street,
London WC1E 7DD,
Broadway House,
Newtown Road,
Henley-on-Thames,
Oxon RG9 1EN and
9 Park Street,
Boston, Mass. 02108, USA
Set in Monotype Imprint
and printed in Great Britain by
Lowe & Brydone Ltd

British Library Cataloging in Publication Data

Hutchinson, Enid

Learning later.
I.   Adult education – England
I.   Title   II.   Hutchinson, Edward Moss
374.9'42   LC5256.G7   78–40271

ISBN 0 7100 8952 x

The Authors dedicate this book
to each other without
whose help it would
never have been written

Contents

Tables

ix

Introduction

Women traditionally have the last word: here I have the first. We each come to this book with a working-lifetime's experience of adult education. This culminated for my husband in a quarter of a century's direction of the National Institute of Adult Education in England and Wales, while I have tutored and organized for thirty years, and I have reflected on and written about that experience both here and abroad. We were both adult students in varying degrees—my husband very much so—in earlier life, and our familiarity with the historic assumptions of the adult education 'movement' reaches back half-a-century.

By the mid-1960s we were both aware that many of those assumptions were no longer valid and that the pattern of English adult education developed around them in the immediate post-war years, although apparently flourishing and occasionally experimental, was failing to meet many emerging needs. The 'generation gap', much talked of at the time, was to a great extent an educational gap. The accretion to the young of educational advantage, hidden to some extent by its uneven spread, operated to the disadvantage of the not so fortunate earlier generations, at work and in the home. The achievement of full employment was bringing married women into the labour market, demanding new adaptations of their skills and opening them up to new ambitions.

The prevailing pattern of adult education, however, was dominated by concepts of leisure-time satisfactions revolving round two-hour, once-a-week commitments to study or activity and this was equally true of local education authority centres and WEA classes as well as of the majority of university-sponsored courses. The new wave of post-war residential colleges had soon settled for a pattern of provision comprising a few days' stay centring usually, also, on a single subject or activity. Sustained and comprehensive study, within the limits of the use of the words 'adult education', was substantially confined to the half-dozen earlier established 'long-term' residential colleges surviving from the pre-war period and able to cater, after the modest extensions of the mid-1960s, for not more than five hundred people annually of whom less than a hundred were women.

So far as there was any new possibility for mature adults to make up for lost or earlier unavailable opportunities it came in the main without intention and in a largely inappropriate form. It was the possibility of piece-meal acquisition of General Certificates of Education, as prescribed for school-leavers, because courses were being provided by student-hungry colleges of further education. Adults who turned to them commonly found themselves in the company of second-go adolescents for whom the courses were primarily intended.

Meeting, teaching and talking to women in WEA classes and Townswomen's Guild groups in the 1950s I was made intensely aware of the apparent and, even more, the latent abilities of the women with whom I came in contact. In 1962, I explored what interest there might be and who might be the takers for a College of the Air that would offer radio support for correspondence courses making sustained intellectual demands and providing a foundation course for women, while they were still homebound with children.[1]

This, however, was only a facet of a larger problem. I was becoming increasingly familiar with the scale of the social and demographic changes that were taking place with profound effects on women's lives. Women were marrying to a degree never experienced in England before and, characteristically, at earlier ages. With this went a new child-bearing pattern that would leave the great majority of women free of the most intense family cares unprecedentedly early. These new familial patterns were not likely to encourage any large number of either men or women to look at residential provision as a remedy for educational insufficiencies. Reviewing a history of Hillcroft College for *Education* in January

1965 I wrote

> But there is only one Hillcroft. In the changed circumstances
> of life today many more women . . . are looking for a 'second
> chance' and . . . must seek it near their homes. Often the
> desire is unformulated. The women flock to the Institutes of
> Further Education and Adult Education Centres, where they
> exist, seeking for much the same mixture of subjects that the
> early Hillcroft students voted for—social studies of all kinds,
> English, literature, art, music and practical handicrafts. . . .
> But they rarely get the advice on planning their studies and
> the oversight of a tutor that the Hillcroft students have. How
> many local authority or voluntary institutes offer a day
> Hillcroft—a foundation course designed to provide, over
> several sessions if necessary, the background of self-developing
> study that creates the confidence to go on to deeper learning
> or professional training? How many provide a student
> counselling service or encourage tutorial relations without
> which such a course cannot hold together?[2]

The chance to put these ideas to the test came a little later when
I was asked by Professor H. A. Jones, then Principal of the City Lit
where I had been teaching English language and literature, part-
time, to help with an extended day-time programme. My recollec-
tion is that when I asked what I would be doing and was told
'more of the same', I found the prospect less than enthralling and
promptly suggested as an alternative a planned composite course
on the lines indicated in my review.

We recount in Chapter 1 how a decision was arrived at in the
time taken to drink a cup of coffee. That the Principal was ready to
seize on the suggestion was a typical example of his own exploratory and innovative attitude. He had made it his business, un-
obtrusively but thoroughly, to get to know his students both day
and evening. He had instituted student advisers to help them to
sort out their expressed and unexpressed needs. It was whilst
working as a part-time adviser that I myself had become aware of
the number of people who were trying to create individual
foundation courses out of the City Lit's separate offerings.

The aim of the new course was to build on this expression of
need by providing, with the help of an integrated tutorial team, a
foundation course as a package deal that would be satisfying in

3

itself but would also encourage the participants to venture into new fields of higher education or training.

So it came about that I designed and directed the Fresh Horizons courses from their part-time day beginnings in 1966, their expansion into evening courses in 1968 and the institution of a full-time course in 1973. Not until that year was I employed other than on a part-time basis and my full-time employment as Tutor-Organizer lasted only a year and a half until I retired from work at the City Lit in 1974. To the best of my knowledge, the Fresh Horizons course, started in 1966, was the first of its kind. Its composition and the way in which the courses developed subsequently, are described in Chapter 1; their essential elements are discussed more fully in Chapters 6 and 7.

But what about the students? From the outset, within the limits of possibility dictated by part-time status and the demands of an otherwise busy life, I kept records derived from their application forms, notes of interviews, letters sent and received and, as far as possible, assessments of work done for the various tutors on the courses. All of this, relating to a total of 388 part-time students, has been drawn on in the ensuing study, together with official records of attendances. This was supplemented by responses to a questionnaire that was sent in 1971 to students on the courses up to that year and, later, to students on courses in 1972 and 1973, a total of 294 being those who substantially completed one of the courses. The same basic information was sought from the first year's 25 full-time students, who are considered in a separate chapter.

The inordinate length of the questionnaire may have deterred some of its recipients from replying—the response rate is discussed in Chapter 9—but this was more than compensated for by the full, frank and often touching character of the responses actually elicited. Indeed the many friendships and encounters made with students both on the courses and subsequently have been a personal delight and an added incentive to complete the present task. It is a great joy to me that so many of them continue to record the satisfaction they have derived from their personal development whether in their social and family life, in their new professions or in their studies at college or university.

I should perhaps make it clear at this point that the research element in the conduct of the courses was a personal and voluntary activity on my part. I had clerical help from the administrative staff of the City Lit and supportive interest from Professor Jones and his successor, Dr R. South, but I had nothing in the way of research grants or other financial support. These facts may suggest a reason, even if they are not offered as an excuse, for any failings in the present work.

To avoid confusion in following the text it may be desirable to set out clearly the course of development. The venture started with one part-time day course, conceived as a whole and requiring two shortened days' attendance over two terms. Within two years, beginning in 1968, an evening course requiring six hours on two evenings was added, and this had to be duplicated as it had in each subsequent year up to 1971. In that year there were also two day courses. In later years twelve-week 'Return to Study' courses on one evening a week were also instituted, particularly for the benefit of accepted entrants to the Open University; except by mention they are not dealt with in this book.

In 1973, the Inner London Education Authority (ILEA), making a major policy shift, asked the City Lit to start a one-year full-time course for which recruited students would be eligible for full maintenance grants, putting them, at that time, on the same footing as students at the long-term residential colleges. The authority was sufficiently satisfied to approve the start of a similar full-time course at Paddington College in 1975. All these courses are still (1978) flourishing, and offered, as they are, both full and part-time, they can satisfy people with different needs and circumstances.

The beneficial outcomes for the great majority of students are analysed in Chapters 3 to 5 and it would be pleasant to record that a major breakthrough in courses of this sort had created a rush of followers and was part of an accelerating trend. Some of the initiatives taken, under a variety of auspices, are cited in Chapter 12 but they have not been prolific and no other local education authority as yet has followed the lead of the ILEA in establishing a grant-aided full-time course of the same kind. Some of the reasons for this are not, unfortunately, far to seek. They are to be found in the inertias of the separated systems of higher, further and adult education; in the regulations governing the allocation of grants to different categories of post-school students; in the increasing diversion of government funds, in the second half of the 1970s, to vocational training schemes thought likely to be immediately relevant to employment prospects and, finally, in the severe cuts enjoined on local education authorities resulting too often in disproportionate reductions in already minimal budgets for adult education.

The Russell Committee had its eyes firmly fixed on the existing scene and, recommending a little more of the same, could only suggest one more residential college, ignoring the possibilities pioneered in the Fresh Horizons approach. During the writing of this book, the Open University Committee on Continuing Education has met and reported. It was properly mindful of the needs of future students for more intensive preparation now that the first large intake of the better qualified has passed through the university's open doors. For this reason, and also because of a more general concern for educational opportunity for adults, it has explored the idea of a loosely conceived Open College system. Based on the existing network of provision, linked by a guidance and counselling system and using a variety of instruments, it would make a more direct approach to what the Russell Committee called the 'quarternary phase' of education. Although aware of the many, mostly short, preparatory courses started for intending OU students, it did not recommend a more comprehensive non-residential 'Fresh Start' approach as a possibly important element in the Open College.

For ourselves we are convinced that it is a concept that, with encouragement, could be extended relatively simply and easily. There are, for example, spread throughout the country some hundred centres in membership of the Educational Centres Association with total annual registrations of the order of 300,000 and they are only part of the vast network of existing facilities, understaffed and underfinanced as most of them are. Fresh Start initiatives have already come from polytechnics, university extra-mural departments and colleges of further education. Twenty or thirty centres, chosen in the first place from this wealth of possibilities and provided with funds to develop courses, counselling services and tutor-counselling training arrangements, could be the beginning of a major new enterprise in adult education.

The need is as great as ever: though the first Fresh Horizons courses were launched on a seemingly rising tide of prosperity, they continue to help people stranded by its ebb. In the meantime the quality of much of our recent provision of compulsory education has been closely questioned and those who have suffered under it will be with us for a long time. The years of easy-come and take-it or leave-it in employment have left an unknown number of adults half-educated and half-trained and with little prospect in life without a fresh start. The pattern of early marriage has left many women under the age of thirty with a completed family and most of a life to fill—and marriage no longer provides a secure livelihood! All in all, as school numbers decline, with children in the descendent, the time is overripe for a new educational deal for adults.

Enid Hutchinson

I have not a great deal to add. I have taken a full part in the preparation of this book, but my wife takes precedence since it is so largely an account of her personal efforts. I, obviously, know better than most people how substantial and demanding those efforts have been and I know a good deal too, at first hand, of the life enhancement that has resulted from them for so many people.

The chapter concerning Fircroft and Hillcroft Colleges, which is my specific contribution, may seem to be only a diversion from the main theme. We think not. The obvious value of these and the other residential colleges has encouraged a very deep regard for them to the point of obscuring the pitifully small numbers they have ever been able to accommodate. I have had a very long personal connection with Fircroft and I welcomed an opportunity in 1974, when I was invited by the Trustees, to review its achievements and to suggest what its role might be over the next decade. The study I made left me in no doubt about the contribution the college has made to individual lives, but I became increasingly doubtful about its continuing relevance to the kind of society we now are. I began to feel that this particular element in educational provision for adults was, even if unconsciously, serving as an excuse for failure to develop equivalent non-residential provision as the only economically feasible way of catering for larger numbers.

I have, myself, in the past queried the possibility of such equivalence. Obviously the experiences cannot be identical but as I came to know Fresh Horizons students from a succession of courses, it was impossible to ignore the identity of expressions used

7

by students from both situations to describe the satisfactions they had obtained.

In the meantime, disruptive action by students and tutors at Fircroft leading to a public enquiry, redundancies and appeals against unfair dismissals, resulted in a two-year cessation of the normal courses and rendered it improbable that they would be resumed in traditional form. Hillcroft is having to accommodate itself increasingly to non-resident students and, like the other colleges in the group, a majority of its students are committed, on entry, to a course of study centred on the acquisition of a specific qualification.

In making these points we have no wish to denigrate what the colleges actually do: what we want to assert is that they provide no answer to the claim that very large numbers of adults stand in need of opportunities to reassess their educational status and their potentiality for growth through learning. We would not think it necessary to labour the point if we did not have before us the example of the Russell Committee described in Chapter 12. So far as we can see the Committee was trapped by its legitimate admiration into quite unrealistic advocacy of residential colleges as meeting the needs of 'the adult who, for whatever reasons, did not take the normal route onwards from school'.

It remains for me to say on our joint behalf that we do not offer this book as directly concerned with the most brutally disadvantaged of our fellow countrymen. Humanitarian and political sympathizers are vigorously trying to fuel the modest flames kindled by the Russell Committee concerning their educational needs, and we have neither desire nor intention to decry their efforts. We have simply observed, over a long period of experience, that large numbers of self-maintaining people in modest employments and women in particular, whether working in or out of the home, live below the level of their learning potential to the detriment of their own happiness and of the public well-being. Unless we seek out, develop and give full play to such under-utilized competence, expressed concern for the most deprived and least competent is too likely to become but a sounding brass and a tinkling cymbal because it is not founded in a wide enough charity—an old-fashioned virtue but, in its true sense, by no means to be despised.

Many sources of assistance are acknowledged by reference in the notes but we are very aware of the less identifiable help that has come from long association and friendship with colleagues in the City Lit, the National Institute of Adult Education, the European Bureau of Adult Education and further afield. It is not invidious, however, to record specially the interest and support of the successive Principals of the City Lit, Professor H. A. Jones and Dr R. South. They will, we are sure, be pleased if we couple with their names that of Mrs P. M. Daley, Deputy Senior Administrative Officer of the City Lit and the members of her staff who cheerfully responded to requests for access to records and the typing and duplicating of forms and questionnaires. Last but not least we offer our grateful thanks to our friend Grace Atkin who, not for the first time, has translated a tangled manuscript into an impeccable typescript.

Edward Hutchinson

I

Fresh Horizons

Premises for adult education come by accident, seldom by design. Like the cast-off clothes of a long family, reach-me-down in the first place and passed on to the last protesting member, such buildings descend the order of educational priorities until, worn and out of date, they survive demolition to supplement, for adult students, their mainstay provision of nightly leavings of younger people's daytime schools and colleges.

Those who involve themselves in teaching adults are accustomed to such makeshifts as they proceed at nightfall to infant schools at the far ends of distant housing estates where their students crouch in junior desks, or to Victorian survivals rescued temporarily from demolition. By contrast, the City Lit in Holborn is that rare phenomenon, a centre where adults actually meet to learn in a place built for them.[1] The site originally accommodated that nineteenth-century by-product of compulsory juvenile learning, a truant school. The purpose-built centre for freely choosing adult learners that supplanted it, still heavily influenced by school design, was opened in 1939, just in time to be pressed into war service. In 1965, it was, in adult education terms, a palace. At that date it had recovered from its war-time commandeering but not entirely from the starkness of austerity. Still groping its way towards the more relaxed interior design and trappings of the 1960s, it was a lively place in which adults could learn and tutors could help them to do so.

About 10,000 students, all part-time, were enrolled every year, some for one class a week, others for any number up to ten. The lower age limit was eighteen, the upper did not exist. They came in the evenings from city shops and offices and in the day-time from homes in London and the suburbs, housewives and retired people, voluntarily partaking of what was, and still is, one of London education's most advanced offerings to its adult population. They made their choices from a range of classes in the humanities, arts, music, drama and languages that, while encouraging the beginner, aimed also to satisfy the more experienced learner.

But in 1965 there was still a restraint on the development of this resource. Pressure on space at other levels meant that the premises were shared by day with that other commonly unrewarded branch of learning, a college of further education. There was, at best, an uneasy co-existence between the sober, zealous adult students and the teenagers, pressured by parents, employers or circumstances, into post-school courses. But more serious than any question of compatibilities was the lack of space for the developing adult programme of the Institute, particularly in the day-time.

It was at the point when the last young people were being seen off into their own premises that one of those innovations was born that are the product of accumulated observations as well as of momentary inspiration. One underlying observation surfaced at the City Lit's annual enrolment period. *Rentrée des classes* for adult education is the early September rush to find out what's happening and where, the study of prospectuses and the penance of queue-forming to join a popular class and pay the fees. In the bustle, tutors try to interview and place prospective students and, at the City Lit, advisers are at the ready to help the puzzled and unsure. It was noticeable, even to an observer only temporarily recruited to advise, that from an *à la carte* offering of a wide assortment of classes, some people were building up courses for themselves—a little English writing practice, a literature class, some history or philosophy.[2] Talking to them, it was clear that, in spite of the City Lit's reputation as an Institute for advanced studies in special subjects, there was a clientele for an extension of general education on a wide front. Approached by interested but uncertain enquirers, advisers might suggest a GCE course at another adult education centre, but the suggestion was often rejected as requiring too close a formalization of scarcely defined needs, or it had been tried without satisfaction. For some, over-impressed by the status of examinations, it was too ambitious; others already had GCEs acquired at school,[3] ten or more years before, of which only a faded memory remained and that were depreciated in value by comparison with the university degrees of friends and colleagues.

The impression gained at enrolment time was reinforced throughout the following months. For several years a rota of advisers, drawn from the part-time tutorial staff, had been on duty each evening to meet enquirers, potential and existing students, to discuss with them their choices of classes and the extent to which they met their needs. Again it was apparent that, for a variety of reasons and from a variety of backgrounds, there were people with needs that were not going to be met by a potpourri of classes, however good they might be as single items. For one thing these people clearly needed someone to show a continuing interest in their problems, a knitting together of tutorial help and consideration not easily obtained when the tutor and the main body of students in a class were immersed in the subject itself and tutors were unrelated to one another except for casual contacts.

There were several possible reasons for the situation in which these people found themselves. Although few of them could have articulated it, they had become victims of educational lag following the extensions of opportunity arising from the Education Act, 1944 and the Robbins Report of 1963. Advertisements for jobs specified 'O' and 'A' levels; graduates were moving into offices and shops; children staying on at school were studying at levels never possible for their parents—the gap between the generations was educational. Perceptive tutors of WEA and other adult classes were aware how often their students of undoubted intelligence and ability, who had left school at fourteen or just beyond, were using their contact with someone in the know to explore the unfamiliar paths their children were treading via the 11-plus to GCEs, sixth forms, college and university. Inherited academic ability or a favourable environment may have been present, but the animating force resided essentially in the parents.

It came as no surprise that many of the anxious enquirers during enrolment periods at the City Lit were women. The family and social pressures that have curtailed the impact of educational advance for girls and the effects on women's lives of the technological and biological changes of the past fifty years are discussed in the next chapter. Adult education outside the vocational field has always attracted a heavy preponderance of women. Many of these were now looking not for 'jobs' but for 'careers', but were we always helping them to open the right doors? Were the people who were trying to build up their own programmes of study getting the right sort of help from the adult education service as it was developing?

Beginning—a day course

A chance to experiment came in 1966 when the young people who occupied the top floor were at last departing to their own premises and new day-time classes could be developed for adults. It was at this point of decision as to how expansion should take place that observation and ideas crystallized. It was quickly decided, indeed within the time of a hasty consultation over a cup of coffee in the canteen, that the next session's programme should include a course of combined studies that would open up for adult students a chance for a fresh start in education. As a new venture, its novelty would lie in challenging the single-subject approach that was currently ubiquitous in adult education outside the half-dozen residential colleges, although it had not gone entirely without challenge.[4]

The chosen elements of the course were English language and literature; social studies; mathematics; speech and drama. If they are to establish new confidence in themselves, language development is as important for adults as it is for growing children. Students had always been attracted to the Effective Speech and Writing classes at the City Lit, so both spoken and written English were seen as necessary elements. English literature, too, is an ever-popular subject, appealing as the medium through which people can most easily extend their imaginations and explore their own and other people's identities. But it is also a means to the development of critical faculties and the analysis of content, ideas and language. The study of society through sociology had not emerged as an expressed demand but students had looked for classes in philosophy and social history as part of their search for greater awareness.

Such were the choices people had made voluntarily, but there was no precedent for including mathematics, not even the new maths, at that time beginning to make its way in the primary schools. To some extent its inclusion was a response to the then

current 'two cultures' debate. The scope of the institution, indicated in its naming as a literary institute, seemed to define the
market, but should not a course of general education offer its
students a chance to recoup on non-literary language skills and
understandings? Lectures on the history of science or the development of scientific ideas would have evaded the reality of grappling
with non-literary modes of thinking and expression. An approach
via experimental science, even if a suitable curriculum could have
been devised, was not possible in a building totally unequipped for
such purposes. The needs of people who were likely, subsequently,
to undertake professional training for teaching or social work had
also to be borne in mind. For many people, women in particular,
the recollections of uneasy hours of school arithmetic and maths
would hover over any decisions to be taken about launching into
training for a career that would include some such elements. But
discussions with prospective students nearly always revealed apprehension about the maths element in the course and it is impossible
to say how many it actually deterred before they got round to such
discussion. The experience of students on this part of the course
was always the most controversial.

There were obvious precedents for including what was at first
called 'Speech and Drama'. There was a need to provide some
physical activity in a tightly packed course. The ability to move and
speak within a larger framework seemed a necessary part of the
development of students moving out of the tight circle of home,
family and neighbours. There is an active Speech and Drama
department in the City Lit with tutors experienced in encouraging
nervous adults to expose themselves in speech and action as a part
of their self-development. So speech and drama and a tutorial
session, completed the weekly programme of the course.

It was essential to the concept of the course that this range of
subjects should be offered and accepted as a package deal. Unlike
the single subject once a week that had become characteristic of
adult education, it was to be a whole undivided undertaking. It
would and could, at that time, only be a part-time course. In the
first place the City Lit was an institution that by administrative
direction was catering exclusively for adults seeking part-time
non-vocational studies. There was also a limit set by the kind of
students it was hoped the course would attract. They would be
mostly housewives venturing outside their home commitments,

who would welcome a chance to do so on a basis that was intentionally demanding but would allow those commitments to come first. What was envisaged was a sufficiently substantial alternative involvement in education to allow such women to experiment with new allocations of their time, to try out, with their families, adaptations of their patterns of joint expectations, demands and activities and to test the feasibility of entering full-time work or study if that was what they were seeking. The course, in fact, catered for the incipient or actual redundancy in the home that many women were aware of but the extent of which they could not gauge except by trial. It was hoped that the course would help them to avoid wrong decisions.

Programme

The programme, as it was first designed, required eight hours of work in class that could conveniently be fitted into two days a week at times fixed to provide for seeing children off to school and being at home when they returned. Allowing for travelling time to central London, this required a 10.45 am start and a 3.30 pm finish. The first timetable was laid out in this way:

Tuesdays	10.45–12.15	Spoken and Written English
Tuesdays	1.00– 2.00	A new approach to Mathematics
Tuesdays	2.00– 3.30	English Literature
Thursdays	10.45–11.45	Tutorial session
Thursdays	11.45– 1.15	Speech and Drama
Thursdays	2.00– 3.30	Social Studies

In later courses the maths period was extended to an hour and a half (making eight and a half hours total attendance) and the lunch break was shortened. Starting time then became 10.30 so that on one day the finishing time was 3 pm. Over the years, students expressed approval not only of the chosen hours but of the selected days. Tuesdays and Thursdays they said were just the days they would have chosen themselves, for Mondays sees the clearing-up after the family weekend, Friday the preparations for the next. The Wednesday break allowed for catching up with mid-week chores and provided time for reading and preparation for Thursday's classwork.

The course was designed to run for two terms, twenty-four weeks in all, from autumn through to spring. Though students often expressed disappointment at the closure of the course at the end of March, the pent-up demands of house and family and the break of the Easter holiday created too much competition to sustain a longer commitment on the part of enough of the group to warrant a continuation.[5]

Prospective students committed themselves on their application forms to undertake reading and written work; discussion in the preliminary interviews stressed that this was no perfunctory requirement. Tutors tried by various devices to ease the reluctance to put pen to paper, but the recruits were left in no doubt that this was the nub of the course. To learn how to read effectively, to use books as tools and libraries as resource centres were to be more important than covering a syllabus or a lengthy reading list. The spate of 'How to study' books was only starting, but Sir Francis Bacon had said what was needed for their guidance as early as 1597 —'Some books are to be tasted, others to be swallowed and some few to be chewed and digested' and had asserted magisterially that 'Reading maketh a full man, conference a ready and writing an exact man'.

Levels

One of the most frequent enquiries about the course was 'What level is it?' so firmly embedded is the idea of grading from eggs and apples to people and their institutions. Even when the numbers recruited led to parallel courses to which students were allocated impartially to course one or two in strict order of acceptance, they still examined each other closely for reasons why they were in one group rather than the other, and sought and found, to their own satisfaction, hidden grounds for streaming. The officials at County Hall were similarly concerned because they graded tutors for pay not by intensity of effort of themselves or their students but, again, by an assumed level. It was difficult in these circumstances for enquirers to accept our assertion that grading, streaming, prior levels of achievement were not now in question. At what age people had left school, with or without what certificate, was subordinate to what they had asked of their lives and what they were prepared to do from now on. Often the reply they received at interview was: 'We shall start with you where you are now—and you are probably further on than you think—and we will take you as far as we can go

in the time we have together and work out the next stage with you.'
This policy did not always succeed with some of the less well-
equipped but many who would have baulked at a programme set to
examination levels did accept the assurances given and found
unsuspected capacities within themselves.

For these reasons the incentive of a diploma or certificate was
rejected. Some students might, subsequently, seek the security of a
qualifying label, but the stick of an examination and the carrot of a
piece of paper would have distorted selection, the conduct of the
course itself and the sort of individual help that was offered as a
part of it. It was not hard to establish these criteria within the
ambience of the City Lit; set up under regulations that excluded
vocational studies and therefore the incentive to build courses that
added units for salary grading, it was accepted that the administration could be permissive and experimental, working with people,
not systems.

But people implies persons and even under a selective system,
when it comes to education, adults are individuals in a way that
schoolchildren are not. Infinitely various as they are, children
grouped by age in classes are homogeneous in comparison with
their parents, grandparents, uncles and aunts, neighbours and the
travellers on the 37 bus. Adults assorted by age, by early education,
by life and work experience come to later education each with a
bundle of attributes, unique and widely various. For the teacher of
adults even more than for the teacher of children, this must imply
readiness to understand the uniqueness of each student as well as
the experiences that members of a group may have in common.
That was why in devising the course, time was made available
within the programme for what was called a tutorial session, from
which arose group and individual counselling. Study problems
were related to home circumstances, husbands, children and the
wider aspects of life in the community and these were common
elements that linked the members of the group. 'I found I was not
alone in having these problems' was a frequent reply to questions
assessing this element in the course as well as 'I found I could
discuss my particular difficulties with the tutor'.

Prospectus and possibilities

The stress on self-development as the aim of the course included
that of self-development with an ultimate vocational goal. The

prospectus description of the course pointed a way in these terms:

A refresher course in general studies for those in mature life who may be thinking of training for teaching, social work or similar professions and who want to test their ability to tackle regular study or to restore their general educational background. Men and women who intend to apply for mature students' scholarships at universities or other establishments of higher education will find it helpful. It will also be of value to people who feel they need a disciplined course of study, suited to their needs as adults, for their personal development or to enable them to meet new circumstances in their lives with more confidence.

The intention is not to prepare for GCE 'O' levels or any other examination and the syllabus for each part of the course will be directed to the personal needs and professional aspirations of the students rather than to examination requirements. No qualifying certificate will be issued and intending students should note that completion of the course does not itself provide an entrance qualification for admission to professional studies.

The course involves attendance from 10.45 am to 3.30 pm on Tuesdays and Thursdays for two terms (27 September to 15 December and 10 January to 16 March, inclusive) together with some regular reading and written work at home.

In addition to the set periods, which all are expected to attend, students will be encouraged, in consultation with the tutor, to make a personal choice of an additional activity— creative writing, painting, music or a foreign language—at a convenient time either concurrently with the main course or in the following term. Help will be given to students in tutorial sessions and through individual counselling to achieve the aims of the course.

This statement defined, to some extent, the kind of students it was sought to serve. Information and counselling extended to job and career possibilities, since these were goals on which many of the students were set. Help in finding out the possibilities that were realistically open to them was as much their need as the process by which they became aware of their potentialities. Fortunately some possibilities did exist: there were openings, for example, for mature entrants to colleges of education. The first year's students made an enquiry, as a class exercise, into the availability of places and the admission policies of such colleges in the region and summarized what they discovered for their own benefit and for that of students on succeeding courses.

It needs to be emphasized, however, that, although job and career counselling was a strong element in the course, it was not predominant. The principal aim was to provide a relevant educational experience that would meet the needs of adults seeking to rebuild or achieve for the first time, a base for their personal learning development, whatever its ultimate outcome.

Evening courses

With the day course established for a couple of years and already proving its value, there came a demand for similar provision in the evenings. This study, therefore, deals also with the evening courses that, beginning in 1968, have run parallel to the day courses in each subsequent year.

From the outset the students on them came from a different level of personal need. Asked what had led them to apply, the housewives of the day courses replied, 'boredom', 'the need to get out of the house', 'didn't want to be a cabbage'. The typists who joined the evening courses were also bored but with their jobs. They lacked mental stimulus in work that demanded little of them. In both groups of students (and if women dominated the day courses almost entirely they were still predominant in the evening courses in a ratio of nearly three to one), there was demonstrated the failure of our economic and social system to develop, extend and use the capacities of the female half of the population.

For four years two parallel courses were held in the evenings, but in 1972 and 1973 the pattern was varied and autumn term 'Study Sessions' of twelve weeks were substituted for one of the courses. This provided a crash course suitable for students who were to start foundation courses of the Open University in the new year and enabled any Study Session students who wished to continue beyond the first term to transfer to the second term of the Fresh Horizons course. A day-time Study Session was also held in 1972 and had some interesting implications but this experiment needed more guidance than could be given while planning for the start of a full-time course in the following year and it was regretfully discontinued.

A major breakthrough

If as the result of a Fresh Horizons course a mother with four children and no school-leaving qualifications went to college, or an ex-typist was reading for a degree in Philosophy, this was not outside the expectations that emerged from time to time from within a conventional WEA or Extra-Mural class. Jude Fawleys have been delivered from obscurity as a by-product of any opening up of late educational opportunity. What was different about the part-time Fresh Horizons approach was that the expectation of such an outcome was written into the prescription and it worked.

But so far this aspect had not led to any need to make a serious adaptation within an accepted framework of provision: though a a larger and more intensive commitment was demanded, the students were surrendering only the margins of their time as housewives or office workers. The tutors, involved as they were beyond the hours and expertise they were engaged for, were part-time, and few out-of-the-way responses were asked of the administration or the budget.

A qualitative change came with the setting up of the full-time course in 1973. It was a recognition by a major public education authority that there was an area of need outside the years of formal schooling and the existing provision made for adults. To enable men and women to give up full-time work for a year of academic study, the ILEA offered discretionary grants to cover fees and maintenance at the full higher education rate and hoped that other authorities would do so for applicants from neighbouring areas. The staff was very clear that this should not be at the expense of the part-time courses as has so often happened in further and higher education. Part-time day and evening courses and the Study Sessions provided variants that met different needs including, for some people, serving as a first step to the full-time course.

The students on the first full-time course blended typical elements of the people attracted to the part-time courses. Women were again the very large majority, twenty-two as against three men, but they included housewives such as might have joined the day-time course and a group of single, mainly young, women who, like the part-time evening students, were clerical workers seeking escape from dead-end jobs.

Neither for the part-time nor the full-time courses, it should be emphasized, were prospective students likely to be deterred solely by the cost of fees. The part-time courses came under the general provision for adult education in the London area for which the fees were a few pounds only—and even so a partial remission could be made at the discretion of the Principal. The full-time course fee of £50 was a more serious matter, but the ready availability of grants for students with the required period of residence within the area of the Inner London Education Authority and the, admittedly more uncertain, grant aid for students from outlying districts meant, in practice, that the cost of fees was not in itself a deterrent. Costs of travel, child-minding, the need for many students to give up work to study even part-time, or for full-time student bread-winners to face living on a grant, were the penalties paid by an adult returning to education, even under favourable conditions.

By 1974, the whole enterprise had attracted some four hundred students into nine day and seven evening part-time courses; the first twenty-five full-time students had completed their year's course and their successors had been recruited. It is now possible to look in some detail at the development of the courses: to see something of their outcome in students' later lives and, with their help, to learn for the future. Since the time when detail on which it is based was collected there have been four more years of student intake.[6] The cursory study of this later period that it has been possible to make does nothing to cast doubt on the representativeness of the students whose experience is recorded or on the general conclusions reached. The next chapter looks more closely at the demographic and social pattern out of which the courses sprang and demonstrates the need for a major policy decision to secure them on a national scale in line with continuing change.

2

Winds of change

It should be emphasized that the changes spelled out here in relation to the period under review are only part of the contemporary and continuing process of change that will take us into the twenty-first century—the century that some have said will belong to the women. Certainly many of the changes have affected women's lives more directly and more intimately than they have men's and this chapter concerns itself with the way in which they have formed a background to the search, particularly by women, for new roles and the means to achieve them.

In the first place they led to a generalized take-up by women of employment and of social and educational activities, although, in the late 1950s and early 1960s, women as a whole made few specific demands for new identities. Nevertheless, by that time there were observers, both in England and in North America, who had become aware that, if women were to emerge into responsible freedom and their abilities were to be properly deployed, their first need was educational re-equipment. The case was argued in educational journals,[1] where the point was also made that the pattern of education, devised for school-leavers, was one that excluded by implication and frequently by direct ruling, women seeking a phased return to education and professional training after a period of child-rearing and home-making.

During the later 1960s and early 1970s there was a growing conscious recognition of these changes and their effects and demands for wider opportunities became more specific and more clearly stated; they were no longer coming only from a vanguard of activists. For the present purpose they are important in that they helped to form the lives of the women described here and provided the urges and motives that brought them together. They are also important because, within any reasonable expectations about the future, they are irreversible. They have permanently affected the pattern of our society and must be taken into account in the continued working of our institutions and in the framing of all future policies.

The changes that are in question are those that stem from revolutionary developments demographically and technologically and their impacts on social and economic life. They have not occurred in isolation and their influence has had multiple effects.

Family women

In the first place, the character of marriage as an institution and an experience, has been affected. More males live to be adults than in the past; fewer have disappeared through war and emigration. Up to the middle years of life there are now more men than women. In contrast to the aftermath of the first holocaust, the young women after the Second World War could confidently expect to lead their men to the altar or, increasingly, to the Registrar's Office. By 1971, 85 per cent of women under 30 were married;[2] between 1951 and 1971, the age of marriage was lowered by nearly two years, and one in three brides were under 20. For their mothers, marriage, a success against odds, usually closed the door on an independent life and livelihood. Marriage secured one's bread and butter and to ensure its safety was a sufficient career; holding a job or pursuing a career outside marriage was the lot of the pitied spinster. Such attitudes went deep into men's and women's assumptions about marriage and can be held to account in part for the tentative approaches many women were making towards the idea of an independent state. They have only been loosened gradually as men and women have lived through their own earlier-started marriages with earlier child-bearing and, as it has turned out, earlier family-completion. In the meantime, the birthrate, reaching its highest modern peak of ninety-three births per thousand women of child-bearing age, in 1964, fluctuated downwards, to the confusion of demographers and planners, to less than seventy-two by 1973. It has dropped further since, and it seems likely from recent evidence that English women are settling for something under two children

23

apiece.[3] The age at which they have or are likely to have them, fluctuates also: of couples marrying in 1961, 43 per cent had no children after two years of marriage; by 1970 that figure had risen to 53 per cent.

Much of this is the effect of conscious and more effective fertility control. The use of the contraceptive pill, beginning in the 1960s, gathered force in the second half of the decade, and, 'by 1973 had become the favoured method of all couples in Britain'.[4] The legalization of abortion in 1967 again reduced the involuntary disruption of women's lives by unsought pregnancies and added to their confidence in seeking enhanced roles for themselves outside the home.

Looser marriage ties were both aided and formalized by legislation on divorce. Between 1961 and 1969, the number of divorces doubled;[5] with the coming into effect of the Divorce Law Reform Act in 1971 they had redoubled by 1972. But while this new legislation on divorce brought freedom, it was often unevenly divided between husband and wife. The period of this study was one in which many more women were facing child-rearing alone. By 1971, over half a million women in Great Britain were bringing up children as lone parents and one in twelve of all dependent children were members of one-parent families. For some of the women students on Fresh Horizons courses their time was filled with the misery of coming to terms with separation and divorce. Taking the course was seen, logically, as a reassessment of their situation, but sometimes it was a blind rush into oblivion of a sort.

Changes in health care have helped to create a fitter and more vigorous female population. Reduced child-bearing, improved treatment for various aspects of gynaecological morbidity, the existence of the National Health Service itself, have combined with better nutrition to increase the life expectation for women at birth, by nearly twelve-and-a-half years since 1931 as against just over ten for men. Chronic sickness rates for women up to the age of 45 in 1971 were below those for men and only when they are very old do they record more limiting long-standing illnesses than men— and far fewer men live to be very old.

Technology and the home

Technological factors, also, have helped to reduce the physical toil of home-keeping, perhaps the biggest single item being the washing-machine in home or launderette. By 1974, 68 per cent of households owned a washing-machine[6] and this, together with quick-drying, minimum-iron fabrics, has noticeably loosened the tie of the kitchen sink. School meals had already reduced the need for mid-day cooking and given many housewives uninterrupted time to themselves during the day. For women in the higher income brackets, the accessibility of a car has eased many aspects of domestic life and increased mobility has opened up opportunities for employment. Women car-drivers holding full licenses increased by nearly one-third in the period reviewed in this study.

The central heating revolution, once the traumas of installation were over, again made for saving of time and toil in house-cleaning. By 1973, two-thirds of better-off households had acquired this advantage, whilst clean-air legislation had begun to reduce atmospheric dirt both inside and outside the home. It was quite noticeable that, for the women on part-time day Fresh Horizons courses, housework, of itself, proved very amenable to reorganization. Some said they became better organized, spent less time on the same work or made adjustments to their work schedules. Others took the opportunity, in anticipation of working outside the home, to buy additional labour-saving tools. It was also in the period of the first phase of Fresh Horizons courses that the spontaneous eruption and wildfire spread of the playgroup move-ment, in itself a response to new conditions, provided a partial relief from the incessant demands of pre-school children, and this was supplemented by the spread of co-operative minding arrange-ments among young mothers.

Attitude changes

Interesting data on national changes in women's attitudes in the relevant period came to light in surveys made by the J. Walter Thompson agency. In 1973 they repeated the terms of a question-naire, originally administered, in 1965, to a national sample of women under the age of 35.[7] It emerged that married women had become substantially less home-centred, and single women, planning marriage, expected to be much less so. The women interviewed in 1973 disagreed more with the statement, 'Working wives can't be good mothers'—only 24 per cent compared to 38 per cent in 1965, endorsed it. Agreement that, 'A woman has as much right to a life of her own as her husband', went up from 47 to 62 per cent. 'Having a job and other interests outside the home' was important for 41 per cent of women whose eldest child was over 5, compared to 28 per cent in 1965. At the same time, preferred leisure-time activities showed a trend away from the home: among those activities, 14 per cent of women with an eldest child over 5, twice as high a proportion as in 1965 expressed a wish 'to be able to study'.

Women were already expressing their new sense of independent possibilities, and taking advantage of eased domestic circumstances, by responding to calls to work from employers who were increasingly prepared to offer part-time work at hours suited to the remaining domestic ties. The proportion of married women in paid employment rose from 10 per cent in 1931 to 40 per cent in 1971, and whereas at an earlier date women had a hard time to find a new job after the age of 40, married or single, by 1971 nearly 58 per cent of married women aged 35 to 54 were working, and were the most economically active age-group among married women.

The women on the first Fresh Horizons course were already tentatively exploring the right to work, some of them armed with copies of *Late Start* (published 1966)[8] or *Comeback* (1964)[9] and BBC programmes for women and women's pages of the quality press were putting the message across throughout the period. The particular emphasis given by the new upsurge of Women's Lib in the mid-1960s had not emerged at the start of the courses. The first day-time students had experienced or observed war-time mobilization of women and were, to some extent, emerging from a late or protracted domestic phase; feminism had, as yet, little place in their search for new outlets. The rediscovery of militant attitudes by an avant-garde sharpened the feminist awareness of later groups, day and evening.

Limitations

But this coin of change had its obverse. Car ownership might have increased, but no tutor on the day courses could fail to be aware of the unease of the mothers of young children as the clock moved to three and the urge to be at the school gates to halt the rush into the busy road became overwhelming. An essay on the topic 'Traffic in Towns' brought replies showing how fear of road accidents dominated the minds of mothers away from their children. Play-groups and co-operative neighbours had their place, but they only freed mothers for an hour or two at a time and there were still school holidays to be covered.

Though changes were far-reaching in quantity they were limited qualitatively. The fact was that, though women now had time on their hands, it was still split-duty time, depending on their capacity to cover the gaps, after school, in the holidays, during sickness and domestic crises. In spite of the controlled family size, children, their health, their welfare, their education and their careers, remained the major concerns of the women with families and created the biggest obstacles to thinking about alternative choices. Attitudes inside marriage had only partially changed; husbands had to be fitted into the picture. It seemed sometimes that, instead of a hundred years ago, Ibsen could only just have written *A Doll's House*. For married women there was a jigsaw of families, husbands and opportunities to be sorted out and the search was on for the employment or training that would fit into the puzzle. But a subtler deterrent has to be reckoned with. The years at home create for women an environment in which the personality develops in a special way. A further adaptation has to take place when the environment is changed and it is helpful if the change is not too abrupt. There are too few part-time education and training courses that can lead into part-time and eventually into full-time work, as children grow into independence.

Single women

The single women who came to the evening courses were them-selves aware of these changes in women's lives in the married state and their attitudes were influenced by them. They were, to some extent, quite consciously preparing for the later stage of their employment as family women, aiming to become better and more flexibly qualified for an ultimate return to gainful employment as well as insuring themselves against dead-end work in the single state. Though their employment and career opportunities did not match up either to their abilities or their educational achievement, they were already, in terms of their school education, below the improving standards for girls of similar capacity who were still at school. If they had left school with 'O' levels, they would, a few years later, have been encouraged to stay on for 'A' levels. Those who left with 'A's had not proceeded to universities as boys might have done in the same years.

Girls still at school were catching up with the boys in 'A' levels[10] and going in increasing numbers and proportions to university: for the non-grammar-school women, the subsequent raising of the school-leaving age to sixteen and widespread adoption of CSE examinations meant that they too were being disadvantaged by time. Even without domestic complications in their lives the problem had to be faced of the limited training and employment opportunities that had potential for women. Frequently the best line of advance was to make use of the increasing number of places at polytechnics and universities, establish a graduate status and so have a better jumping-off ground for the future. The setting up of the full-time Fresh Horizons course in 1973 helped towards this, making it possible to offer, with grant aid, a fuller preparation, on terms not too onerous, even for women with children.

What comes out of any exploration of the paths taken by boys and girls after leaving school is that they are sex-determined. Such changes as are taking place in the schools to overcome sex-linked disadvantages (and many schools still make the commercial course for girls a desirable option), do not prevent girl school-leavers from entering a world where employers' attitudes remain largely undisturbed. Employer encouragement of further education and training is strictly for the boys: between 1966 and 1972—years which are already yielding new entrants to current Fresh Horizons courses— male students on part-time day courses at grant-aided institutions accounted for 20 per cent of the male population of 18- to 20-year-olds; girls never reached 3 per cent.[11] Figures are similar for the 15- to 17-year-olds, except that the percentage for girls rises to 6.

So far as single women, on the courses under review, were preparing for future employment, they were making good deficiences of earlier opportunities, refreshing their learning skills and building on developed expertise to explore new possibilities of education or training at higher levels outside the fields of their present or, currently, possible employments. Apart from a few working in situations with open promotion possibilities into middle management—and these did, in fact, make career headway— current employment offered little in the way of career prospects: they had to get out to get on.

In spite of fundamental changes affecting human procreation, the family and traditional economic and social roles, we are still far from rebutting the words of a government statistician from whose researches this chapter has drawn, that 'A person's sex influences the type of upbringing in the family home, the education experienced, the employment opportunities available and the whole life style of the adult'.[12]

Men

It can be agreed that most of 'the widespread changes in social conditions and attitudes in this century have affected women more than men' but there has been at least one notable exception— the comparatively large extension of post-school further education enjoyed by boys and men in the past twenty-five years, almost entirely related to their work. It was not this development, however, that brought men to Fresh Horizons courses. They were more likely to have taken a wrong turning on leaving school, to have made a mistaken career choice or to have missed their footing on a promotion ladder. Sometimes they were seeking to overcome persistent learning difficulties that had hitherto hampered their progress. Sometimes they were making a deliberate attempt to leave an occupation that was not without prospects, in search of new occupational satisfactions related to interests developed in maturity. But for most married men this is too great a risk to take: few could make use of the day courses and single men predominated markedly in the evening ones. Tightly enmeshed in their roles of breadwinners, married men are much less likely to be able to opt for a complete career change. Redundancy (an increasing factor since 1974) forces it on some and released wives have been known to make it possible for others. On the whole, so far as men are involved in some form of adult education it is much more likely to be career related. This is so whether it is promoted by employers, industrial training boards, the Department of Employment or by the WEA or university extra-mural departments in courses for shop stewards and trade unionists.

Induced social change

Apart from demographic and technological changes and their social consequences, the situation that is created by deliberately induced social change has to be reckoned with. To have engineered a set of changes and applied them solely to the emerging new generations of children and young people while leaving the established population to cope as best it may will be seen as the ultimate failure of our legislators and administrators.

It is only necessary to list some of the changes consequent on the extension of secondary, further and tertiary education to measure the disadvantage created for those who were regarded as having received, at an earlier stage, their educational equipment for life. That so many of them were unaware of this, or, being aware, coped, is no excuse for the ignorance of the engineers.

Two successive raisings of the school-leaving age immediately disadvantaged those who had left school in the preceding years. Increased opportunities—the growth in sixth forms and higher education provision; the extension of further education and day-release facilities; the introduction of the Certificate of Secondary Education—have all contributed to the advantage of today's younger generation. But the advantage has not been uniform: it has been gradually, often sporadically determined and subject to the accidents of time and place.

Information collected by the National Institute of Adult Education from a substantial population sample in the late 1960s already showed the process at work as is illustrated by the extract from a larger tabulation which forms Table 1.

A later illustration, expressed in terms of educational qualifica-

Table 1 *Proportions of three age-groups leaving school at specified ages (sample c. 1966–7).*

		age-groups		
		18 – 34	35 – 54	55 and over
	N =	949	1,370	1,224
left school at		%	%	%
15 or under		59	78	84
16		20	10	5
17 and over		19	13	12

Source: Provision for Adult Education - Table G 3 (NIAE, 1970)

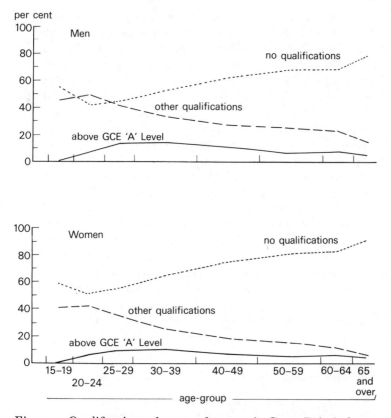

Figure 1 Qualifications of men and women in Great Britain by age group. (Source: *General Household Survey, Introductory Report*, HMSO, 1973, p. 245, reproduced with the permission of the Controller of Her Majesty's Stationery Office.)

tions acquired, is provided by Figure 1.

The Russell Committee report also made the point:

The pressures of our society, which create or exacerbate the needs from which these demands emerge, set up a Darwinian situation in which the educationally fittest survive. But they are a minority. Almost three-quarters of the adult population left school at the minimum leaving age; three-fifths of today's adults received their schooling before the leaving age was raised to fifteen; better opportunities for technical education

31

and the broadening of entry into further and higher education
came too late to benefit them; and the fresh approaches to
education that are transforming many schools, notably
primary schools with whole new dimensions of educational
experience, are unknown and inaccessible to all but today's
children. Government statements over the years have testified
to serious deficiencies of accommodation and staffing in a
number of the nation's primary and secondary schools,
particularly those in sub-standard dwelling areas. Research
has demonstrated the advantages in rate of educational
development that lie with children from the 'better' school,
to say nothing of the 'better' home, and has shown that a
substantial number of persons, because of their biological
make-up, attain much later than others to the ability—often
then of a higher order—for academic or creative work, social
work or leadership. It cannot be in the interests of justice or
the efficient use of human resources that numbers of our
fellow citizens now find themselves too late at the gates of
wider opportunity, and with no further recourse.
Educationally we are still Two Nations, and among the
educational 'have-nots' the needs are vast.[13]

Not only employment

Neither for men nor for women, however, were the courses aimed
wholly at fresh horizons in employment. The upsurge of educational
opportunity since the war through the expansion of universities,
the widening of curricula, the added years in schools and the
developments in further education already mentioned, have all
contributed to a steady increase in demand for adult education at
all levels. More money to spend, foreign holidays, challenges to
parental attitudes from more sophisticated youngsters, have all
stimulated mature adults to explore unknown ways. For the better
educated young people entering maturity they have encouraged
marked changes in traditional life-styles. It is symptomatic of this
that the J. Walter Thompson survey mentioned above shows s
young married population moving from beer to wine and from tea
and buns to coffee and sandwiches in its entertainment patterns.
Young married women, in particular, are shown to be more out-
going in their leisure interests—knitting, watching television and

other indoor activities show a decline, with parties, drinking and outdoor recreation taking their place. In adult education centres, the interest in wine-making and wine-tasting classes, in continental cookery and holiday languages reflected this trend. The enforced austerity latterly created by wage restraint and inflation may affect this pattern, but habits and expectations have been established that will hardly allow it to be destroyed.

People drawn to the City Lit are among those consciously in search of cultural satisfactions, and responsive to the changing intellectual climate of their time. For some of these the opportunity of intensive study afforded by the Fresh Horizons course created a new plateau from which they could launch themselves. Some of them, in doing so, also found new careers; for others the reality of the experience was summed up in the words of a student who left school thirty years before at the age of fourteen:

'I am treated seriously as a person as well as a parent since the course. As a result of improved self-confidence I am more positive in my work and therefore more efficient. I would like to see all Shakespeare's plays and make the theatre part of my life. My social life is beautifully enlarged with City Lit friends.'

Under threat?

The trends and their implications discussed here are only likely to be reversed in the near future as a result of catastrophic upheaval, but one change since the late 1960s and early 1970s is outstandingly important and should be noted. The early years of the Fresh Horizons courses were years of plentiful employment opportunities, particularly in the London region: throughout the country generally there was a low unemployment rate and a surplus of vacancies over applicants. In 1976, for the first time since the 1930s, the registered number of unemployed exceeded one million and they were no longer confined to 'depressed areas' and 'heavy industry'.

In such a situation (and it has worsened since) women's emergence into a larger sphere of activity is under threat. Traditionally regarded as a useful reservoir of unskilled or semiskilled labour in times of national need and with career fulfillment interrupted by the domestic interlude in their lives, they are seen as easily dispensable. Figure 1 shows also the extent to which they are further disadvantaged as a sex by a qualification lag—itself a reflection of social attitudes that trail behind social change.

The implications of a changing situation for adult education generally, are discussed more fully in Chapter 12. But does a recession mean that women will beat a forced retreat to the home? Their roles have been changing for the past two centuries since the impact of the first industrial revolution. The years of militancy that have recurred at intervals mark the points at which conscious recognition of change has erupted. There have been advances and retreats but, in the main, the forward movement has been maintained. If, in the future, the wind of change comes from a new quarter, it will blow on a scene already set by the changes outlined here. Wives and mothers, in recent years, have exchanged unpaid leisure in the home for paid work outside it and the better educated and more consciously directed among them have sought to use their abilities in more responsible and fulfilling jobs. For the moment some of them may have become teachers only to discover that the movement out from the home, of which they are part, means that there are fewer children to teach.

But there can be no return to the *status quo ante*. Women will not forgo their washing-machines nor will manufacturers want them to do so. The problem still remains: how do we organize ourselves, as a community, to make the best use of the human resources represented by women's capacities? Their intelligence provides at least half the world's total brain power. In the industrially advanced countries it is no longer needed exclusively for the rearing of today's smaller families and the maintenance of increasingly mechanized homes. The management skills, always implicit in women's traditional functions, are now for sale to a larger world. It is the task of our educational system to ensure that the education and training necessary for their full utilization are made available and for industry, commerce and administration to recognize the value of the resources they are, at present, largely ignoring.

3
Part-time day students

In the preceding chapter some indication has been given of the social and demographic changes that have helped to create the recognition of a need, particularly by women, to extend the range of their lives. Yet, on the whole, the women described in the following pages felt this need intuitively rather than explicitly. To this extent they were typical products of their time rather than otherwise. Yet, out of a street, an office block, a housing estate, they were out-of-the-ordinary in that they not only felt their need but they responded to a challenge. Nor could they be categorized. Some students certainly typified recurring features in the recruitment—housewives whose youngest child had recently started school, for example, or city secretaries, under-employed in relation to their abilities—but each course brought together a group of people diverse as to age, education, and experience of work and living.

This survey is concerned with the total number who enrolled in day and evening part-time courses from their inception in 1966 until and including the 1973–74 session, of whom there were 388 excluding a small number who made a brief encounter at the start of a course but left before the expiry of a three week period that entitled them to go on to the permanent register. Of the registered 388, women numbered 310, of whom 168 were day and 142 evening students. Only 20 men attended at any time during the day and 58 in the evening. Throughout the years recruitment has been limited only by the number of places available.

A feature of the day courses that is apparent even in the brief histories that follow is that, over the eight-year period, the women students became younger. On the first course there were no students under 35, but in 1970 half of them were under that age and, though in succeeding years the proportions varied, the later day-time students were characteristically in the 30–39 age-group rather than the 40–49 of the early courses. But the courses throughout continued to attract some women in their late 40s or 50s and over who were keen to meet a new learning challenge.

Table 2 *Registered part-time students—percentages in specified age-groups*

	women				men		
	day	day	day	evening	day	evening	
	1966–9	1970–3	total	1968–73	1966–73	1968–73	total
age-groups	N=76	92	168	142	20	58	388
	%	%	%	%	(N)	%	N
1–24	1	4	3	19	(4)	16	46
25–29	1	7	4	29	(4)	21	64
30–34	12	29	21	15	(4)	20	73
35–39	19	21	20	12	(2)	22	65
40–44	28	17	23	8	(2)	9	56
45–49	19	11	14	11	(2)	5	45
50–54	11	4	7	4	–	2	18
55 and +	7	7	7	2	(2)	5	19
Not known	2	–	1	–	–	–	2

Women by day—first phase

Of the 168 women who joined the part-time day courses, 105 returned the questionnaires sent to them. These show that, until the 1970 course, the students had, with only five exceptions, left school before or during the Second World War. They form a group of 44 women aged thirty-five and over, and, because they are so much the products of a different history and social scene, it is worth considering them apart from younger and later students.

Their earlier educational history is subsumed in Table 3 in the details for all respondents who attended the day courses, 1966–9 as in this respect the figures for the 44 differ very little from those for the 49 of which they comprise so much the larger part.

Table 3 *Respondents—types of school attended and terminal ages of full-time education (percentages)*

		women				men
		day			evening	evening
		1966–9	1970–3	total	1968–73	1968–73
early education	N =	49	56	105	53	27
		%	%	%	%	%
schools attended						
elem./sec. modern		20	20	20	21	59
central/technical		16	11	13	11	7
grammar/comprehensive		39	39	39	38	15
private—day and boarding		25	30	28	30	19
terminal age of full-time education						
under 15		12	20	16	13	30
15		16	14	15	23	34
16		29	23	26	28	11
17		25	20	22	15	3
18 and over		18	23	21	21	22

A few brief histories tell something about individual women who joined the first courses:

A.B. Born 1912. Aged 54 at start of course in 1966. Married with two teenage children at home. Housewife for more than twenty years. Telephonist previously. Won scholarship to grammar school but left at 16 just before matric because of family needs. Took speech training and drama at London evening institutes over the years. Was already planning a way back to work and therefore 'welcomed the opportunity' to test her ability through the Fresh Horizons course then starting up. She worked part-time first as the secretary of a voluntary society and then as a library assistant for ten years until retirement only regretting that there were too few opportunities for education and training when she started afresh.

C.D. Born 1921. Aged 45 at start of course in 1966. Married with two late teenage children at home. Housewife for twenty years. Office jobs until marriage. Left pre-war central school at 14. Had two goes at learning foreign languages at evening classes, also painting and drama but had social and political interests that at the time of the course led her into teaching first an adult illiterate and, after the course, into part-time remedial teaching at a school of which she was a manager. Seeing the need for professional training, she entered a college of education via the special entry test at the age of 49 and became a qualified teacher.

E.F. Born 1919. Aged 49 at time of the course in 1968. Married but daughter already grown up and away from home. Had worked in a factory on leaving elementary school at the age of 14. Went into RAF during the war and afterwards became a factory security officer until she retired in 1960. She then developed an absorbing passion for pottery and painting which she studied part-time. Her aim in taking the Fresh Horizons course was to extend her general educational background and gain confidence in speaking and writing so as to extend her art interests. Since then has had her own studio built and equipped, sells her pots and paintings, gives talks to women's groups and teaches in a further education college, having gained qualifying certificates including a City and Guilds Teachers' Certificate.

G.H. Born 1924. Aged 43 when on the course in 1967. Housewife with three teenage children. After three years' war service in WRNS had trained at RADA and was on the stage for two years. At 16 got good School Certificate in spite of attending six different schools in three countries. After Fresh Horizons course helped in a youth club and did an 'A' level when her children did theirs. Trained as a social worker 1972–4 and is now senior medical social worker in a teaching hospital. Says the first step—into Fresh Horizons—was the hardest to take.

I.J. Born 1922. Aged 47 at time of the course in 1969. Married with four teenage children. Full-time housewife and mother, after serving during the war as ATS officer. Left independent boarding school at 17 with five credits in School Certificate. Attended oil painting and Laban movement classes at local adult institute. Following Fresh Horizons did four-year part-time course at a college of education and is now a nursery school teacher.

Only six of the forty-four women referred to earlier left school at the appropriate minimum leaving age of 14. This placed them among the educationally more fortunate of their generation, three-quarters of whom had minimum schooling. Over a quarter finished school at 16, compared to 11 per cent of their contemporaries, and nearly half of this number left at 17 or over as against 7 per cent of the population at large. Over one-third had a pre-war school certificate or matriculation exemption compared with something like 6 per cent in the total population. Even so this means that two-thirds of them left school without an entry ticket to a professional training and, by 1966, much higher entry qualifications than those that satisfied earlier criteria were already being required of would-be late entrants.

War-time disruption had played a part in this. One student wrote, 'War-time evacuation, prevented me taking a place at a grammar school. I lost the advantage a good education would have given me. I left school at fourteen after spending four years at a variety of schools, mostly housed in inadequate premises.' Others wrote, 'I couldn't take the eleven-plus scholarship' and 'couldn't matriculate' was mentioned four times. Of thirty-two women in this group who replied that their earlier education had been disrupted, fourteen attributed it to war and evacuation, the largest single cause quoted. The next largest was family removals, some of these also being related to war-time conditions.

Nevertheless, thirty-four of these forty-four pre-war and war-time school-leavers claimed some kind of *post*-school education leading to possession of a diploma or certificate. A few had dual qualifications, e.g. SRN and a commercial training. In fact, in relation to the time when they left school and were launched into earning, their parents probably felt they had given them a good start. In the main they had a full-time commercial training for no more than three-to-twelve months or had obtained typing and shorthand certificates by attending evening classes, but full-time training for the army, the navy, the stage and the kitchen are represented in the figures.

Table 4 *Respondents—post-school education leading to certificates, etc.*

		women				men
		day			evening	evening
		1966–9	1970–73	total	1968–73	1968–73
type of certificate	N =	49	56	105	53	27
			2(pt)	2 (pt)		1 (pt)
1 degree*		1	1	2	–	–
certificate/diploma full-time study						
2 commerce		9	9	18	7	–
3 other		6	9	15	9	2
4 nursing		4	4	8	2	–
5 part-time study		9	5	14	9	8
as mature students†						
6 GCE		6	4	10	3	2
7 other		4	2	6	–	2
having some qualifications		37	36	73	30	15
% of N having some qualifications		75%	64%	69%	56%	56%

* With one exception the degree studies reported were pursued abroad.
† Lines 1–5 above relate to further education end-on to school. Lines 6 and 7 relate to studies resumed in later life.

For ten of them, post-school education was wholly that taken recently, mainly leading to GCE certificates prepared for by correspondence study or at adult classes. But qualifications obtained as adults included an air-pilot's licence, speech and drama certificates and ballroom dancing gold medals.

In brief, the women on the first courses had, on the whole, received a school and immediate post-school education or training that served them for earning a living in minor white-collar occupations during the 1940s and 50s. Some of them had already sought fresh starts as mature adults in what was available through specialist interest qualifications and GCE examinations.

What else were they finding on offer in the adult education provision of the time? It has been unfortunate that, in what development there has been in adult education since the Education Act, 1944, there was little concern for renewal education for those whose schooldays were well behind them or were interrupted by the war. 'Serious' adult education was largely confined to non-certificate-seeking WEA and university extra-mural classes. London university made a relatively substantial offering of part-time diploma classes in the humanities, related mainly to the interests of teachers and white-collar and professional workers in limited fields; similar offerings were very thin on the ground elsewhere.

The undoubted demand for classes related to domestic skills or in arts, crafts, physical activities and foreign languages, created an image of local education authority adult education that came to be described, with initial encouragement from the Department of Education, as 'recreational'. Because of the mainly utilitarian attitude to educational spending this often became a denigratory term even though, at the same time, more money and time were being expended, within the formal years of school education, on these very subjects—arts, crafts, music, games.

Their popularity with adults who had known a sparser regime in their pre-war and war-time schooling, perhaps tended to obscure the need for renewal education in basic terms. As colleges of education began to open their doors to mature entrants to meet the teacher shortage, they were limited in what they could suggest by way of preparation to a GCE course at a college of further education or a WEA class.

The first Fresh Horizons students—and it applies equally to later ones—were by no means neglectful of the adult education opportunities around them: only nine had failed to make some use of them. Over the years they had done their keep-fit, pottery, art, cookery, language or WEA classes. Within the group, twelve women recorded involvement in 'conceptual' and twenty-four in 'activity' classes.

Few of these first students were working outside the home when their Fresh Horizons course started: seven had part-time jobs, mostly clerical. As girls they had, in the main, entered employments of lower standards than their education warranted and the break in continuity caused by marriage and child-rearing reduced their status on returning to work. In their first jobs, three-quarters of them were in clerical occupations of the kind described by the

Registrar-General as 'junior non-manual'. Only one, a doctor seeking new interests in retirement, was in the official 'professional' category. The 'intermediate non-manual' group that covers the remainder, consisted of a few nurses and former actresses. By contrast not many of their husbands were in the same classifications: four-fifths, in fact, were recorded as having professional or managerial jobs. This did not mean that the women had married upwards in the social sense, but that, from the start, they had been employed downwards.

Thirty-eight of these early-course women had children living at home and although the average number of children for the group was 2·5, four of them—extremely vigorous women, used to full, demanding lives—had families of five or more. As a whole this group were less immediately prompted than later students to fill a gap as their children started school; their children were more likely to be entering secondary rather than primary school; only a third of the children as compared with one-half later, were under 10. These were the families of the 'bulges' of the 1940s and 50s, of post-war family building and national austerity, just emerging into the new climate of the late 1960s.

Table 5 *Respondents (women day-students)—numbers and ages of children at home*

course years	number women	average number	Children			
			numbers in age-groups			
			—5	5–10	11–17	18 and +
1966–9	38	2·5	4	30	43	20
1970–3	39	2·25	3	44	24	17

The picture of the earlier groups of women day-students that emerges is of members of a generation who had been educated before or during the Second World War—decidedly better educated on the whole than most of their peers—but having missed opportunities to qualify to the level that might have been expected but for war-time disruptions and family and societal assumptions about their roles as women. They had been plunged into the intensities of family life during the post-war period, taking what opportunities there were, within the developing adult education service, to learn craft and other skills in their time out. They were, for the most part, comfortably off, with husbands of higher occupational standing than they themselves had been accorded. Their children were now launched into school life, mostly in secondary schools.

What then induced them to seek a fresh horizon? The reasons they give—'boredom', 'time on my hands'—are not sufficient explanation by themselves for their response to an invitation to go beyond what was available in neighbourly contacts, women's clubs, voluntary work, the offerings of traditional adult education and the low-status occupations for which they had initially been prepared. The reasons why escape into superior employment offered itself as a solution to the post-war *ennui* experienced by many women are properly sought in the character of economic and social change with their special impacts on women's lives that are discussed in Chapter 2.

Not all, but a considerable proportion, of these early women students certainly made decisive changes in their ways of life. The main outlet after the part-time day course, at that time, was the college of education. Of the married women on the first four courses who completed the questionnaires, one-quarter went into teacher training. Five are known to have taken jobs without further training, three as part-time librarians. More would have trained as social workers had places been available, but two, after some years of further voluntary work, did manage to get on to courses. Some made their way, via language or craft skills, into further education or adult teaching, sometimes with the help of City and Guilds certificates. Two were subsequently enrolled for Open University degrees. Table 6 shows the outcome regarding subsequent education for all the women on these early courses who responded to the questionnaire.

Women by day—second phase

Table 2 shows the movement down into younger age-groups during the years 1970–3. More than a quarter of the students in that period had started school after the war and most of the remainder had been in primary rather than secondary school during the war years. Some of them recall war-time upheavals, e.g. 'We were continually moving house during the war and schools too—I took no serious exams and finally left school (private day) at fifteen'; 'Due to the war I had no real schooling until I was eight. Between seven and twelve years there was lack of continuity and homesickness on evacuation. When back in London for intermittent periods, the school was closed'; 'During the war I lived in London and quite a lot of our school-time was spent in air-raid shelters and under desks; very little teaching was done'. But a student who had an orphanage upbringing wrote, 'Evacuation was for the better. We attended a modern school in Nottingham where the standard was higher and the school went in for musical activities. We performed *Iolanthe*, a high spot.'

Brief biographies may, again, convey something of the characteristics of this later group.

K.L. Born 1945. Aged 26 at time of course in 1971. Married but as yet no children. Had just finished work as air steward and had previously tried nursing, and worked as an audiotypist, hotel receptionist and medical secretary. Left independent school at 17 with eleven 'O' levels. Says 'I did not want to do "A" levels and was not encouraged to do so. I think with more encouragement I would have done them and obtained qualifications I later lacked. However, the variety of work I have done now proves to be a valuable experience.' After school life took part-time classes in typing, modern dance and a course on contemporary problems. During Fresh Horizons course was encouraged to apply to a local university, but as 'A' levels were insisted on, left the course to work at home by correspondence while keeping in touch for counselling. She obtained a First Class Honours Degree in 1975 taking finals when four months pregnant. 'My husband is pleased that I went to university and I feel more fulfilled.' In the meantime she is casting round for part-time lecturing and tutorial work to fit in with family ties.

M.N. Born 1941. Aged 30 at time of course in 1971. Married with two children aged 12 and 10. Full-time housewife but had previously run own business. Left school at 18 with eight 'O's and three 'A's and married almost immediately. Did not attend any classes post-school. Following the course she started studying for a law degree after much careful consideration but writes 'There was lack of support from my husband—at first mental and physical and then purely physical—he had no time to help me run the home. The grant I received did not allow me to have sufficient outside help. I felt that our whole family relationship was crumbling and that my family was more important to me than a career even when my husband's attitude turned to pride.'

O.P. Born 1920. Aged 51 at time of course in 1971. Married with teenage and grown-up daughters at home. Full-time housewife for twenty-seven years. Left elementary school at 14 to work as dress machinist and during the war as storekeeper in an aircraft factory. Took part-time evening classes in psychology, languages, speech and pottery at intervals over twenty-three years. Though she joined the Fresh Horizons course for interest and personal satisfaction she followed it up by taking an 'O' level English securing an 'A' grade in the examination. Later she took a TOPS course in office skills and is working in a personnel department. She records her 'surprise and delight as children realised I was more than just Mum who cooked and baked, especially my rebellious teenage daughter who was studying the same books as I was for her "A" level sociology.'

Q.R. Born 1941. Aged 31 at the time of the course in 1972. Married with three children (10, 8 and 7). Full-time housewife for ten years. Previously bank clerk, one year and dental nurse, four years. Left grammar school at 16 with three 'O's. Says 'My parents felt education was unimportant especially for a girl. I feel now that this attitude and the conflicting values of my home (which was working class) and the school created difficulties. Some mornings I would arrive at the school gate and just couldn't face going in. As a result I plummeted from the A class to the lowest grade. With the taste of failure in my mouth I gave up trying and spent five years of misery. I felt my experience at grammar school created a series of barriers which were not finally overcome until I came to Fresh Horizons.' Tried a pottery class at an evening institute in the meantime. After the Fresh Horizons course she spent a year taking part-time 'A' level classes in sociology and English and obtaining a C grade in the former. Started a degree course at a polytechnic in 1974. Says 'My husband didn't like me studying in the evenings (he still doesn't) but has developed more interests of his own and now goes to art classes. We compensate for this by going out more regularly. We both feel our time together is more precious because it's limited.'

It will be apparent that as a whole these later students were very similar in childhood education to the earlier ones, although one in five as opposed to one in eight had left school at or below what had become the minimum leaving age of 15. The remainder were better equipped with school-leaving certificates (see Table 8) than the women on the earlier courses but their immediate *post*-school education differed little from that of their predecessors. More of them, about one-third, had already returned to work, almost entirely into part-time, largely junior, clerical jobs. Their first work had been mainly clerical, but recruits came also from other and varied fields. Medical social worker, theatrical costume maker, cartographer, dress machinist, estate agent, air steward, were some of the former callings of women on these courses, all of whom had reason, in the prevailing circumstances of their lives, to reassess their capacities and aims for the future. Some students, on the other hand, had no experience of employment outside the home, having married straight from school. There were also more heads of single-parent families in this later group, ten out of the total of fifty-six women and a quarter of the thirty-nine with children at home. More of them, too, had children in the primary stage of education. Single women, without children, included two secretaries who were living on savings and some part-time work, a musician preparing for a teaching career and a retired woman, simultaneously training to be a London guide.

Outcomes

With the development of CNAA courses at London polytechnics, it was becoming more possible, towards the end of the period under review, to get a place on a degree course without traditional entry qualifications, so a few more of the later students were able to consider this as a possibility. The outcome of the courses in relation to subsequent education and training, as they developed for both the later and the earlier groups, can surely be considered remarkable.

In summary thirty-seven women went on to full-time higher

education of one to four years' duration; nineteen took up part-time study leading to a qualification (other than GCEs) including five who registered with the Open University and followed the course with further part-time studies at the City Lit and elsewhere. Some of those pursuing part-time studies were in full-time or part-time work. The details are spelt out in Table 6.

Table 6 *Respondents—educational activities after completing Fresh Horizons courses*

educational activities	women				men	
	day			evening	day	evening
	1966–9	1970–3	Total	1968–73	1966–73	1968–73
university level						
conventional	2	8	10	8	–	8
Open University	2	3	5	8	1	2
college of education	11	9	20	8	1	4
social work training	4	1	5	3	–	–
full-time adult education	1	1	2	1	1	1
further education qualifications	8	6	14	3	1	1
GCE 'A' and 'O' levels	9	6	15	8	1	2
non-certificate courses	20	17	37	11	2	7
number of respondents	49	56	105	53	7	27
number reporting activities	43	51	94	46	5	21
percentage reporting activities	88	91	90	87	(5)	78

Some respondents record taking more than one course after 'Fresh Horizons', e.g. GCE and OU.

Of the non-respondents it is known that at least one in four was engaged in substantial educational activity. This is certainly an under-estimate of the numbers actually doing so.

What of the others? It is obviously desirable to attempt to assess the value of the courses for those who did not subsequently take up study leading to a qualification or re-enter the working world by reason of age, family commitments or inclination. Participants were asked:

'Are you aware of any subsequent effects of attending the Fresh Horizons courses as far as home, family, work and social life goes?'

and

'Are you aware of any change in yourself and your range of interests (other than those recorded here) since taking the course?'

There were replies from twenty-four respondents who had not entered on certificate-seeking full- or part-time further education, and they illustrate the variety of needs to be met and the responses elicited, e.g.

'It got me out of a rut I seemed to drown in. Continuing to attend courses at the City Lit keeps the mind occupied.'

(Retired professional woman)

'I am not so complacent: at my age I found it challenging. It has alerted me.'

(Woman of 54)

'I attended two market research meetings: I felt I was able to hold my own and summarise at the end.'

(Housewife undergoing mental stress)

'Increased confidence has enabled me to project myself into activity which I did not realize I could do before, like trying new recipes, new ideas.'

(Housewife aged 45)

'Through your advice I went further afield and much enjoy my voluntary work in the nearby town. Thank you.'

(Housewife aged 55)

'I think I am more tolerant with my children regarding their homework and not so inhibited about entering into discussion with my friends. I enjoy and get more out of reading and am not so sensitive about my lack of education. I have been to art exhibitions and very much enjoy teaching my illiterate student to read and spell.'

(Middle-class housewife; SRN; left school at 14)

'I was able to bring home new ideas to my family. I would

like to follow up subjects which I have been introduced to for the first time in my life.'

(East European refugee; left school in Hungary at 14)

'I was helped to decide against taking an Open University course, but given plenty of ideas for studying and appreciating English literature and will enter WEA courses whenever possible.'

(Woman moving out of London on retirement of husband)

'My course of study has given me a more intellectual attitude towards my painting. I was trained to be a visual artist but have discovered that the approach to painting can not only be a visual one. . . . I expect to go on learning through painting for the rest of my life: I find this a very interesting and stimulating prospect.'

(Housewife, artist and mother)

It has frequently been suggested that vast fields of voluntary endeavour lie to the hands of supernumerary housewives and that these should provide adequate outlets for their energies and abilities. The Fresh Horizons students showed themselves responsive to demands for service to the community as part of their normal way of life. Thirty-nine of the respondents were engaged in some kind of voluntary work when the course started and although fifteen of them did not continue because, in the main, of involvement in full-time study, another fourteen started voluntary work after the course ended.

But it is no answer to the needs of these women to point to the demand for voluntary workers. Community service, at the directing level, is increasingly the province of professionally qualified personnel, and volunteers feel that their tasks are circumscribed, demanding only the lower levels of domestic and clerical skills from which they are trying to escape. Moreover, for many housewives, voluntary work is a luxury they can only afford to a limited extent, demanding as it does not only an outlay of time but of money for fares or petrol. The time itself is not grudged if capacities are being employed at a level that allows for the development of the worker as well as for the smooth running of the organization. The popularity of youth work, drama, playgroup activity and work with illiterates, among members of these groups was perhaps part of their general interest in educational satisfactions.

49

The outcome of the course, at the time of completion or at a given moment later, is not necessarily final. Five or more years afterwards, former students have been known to write for a reference, to announce an intention that has been simmering since the course ended, or to talk over prospects now that subsequent full-time education has been completed. For many people the experience of the course has set something in motion, the exact character of which is often difficult to trace, but which has influenced and, perhaps, changed, the direction of their lives.

Men by day

Nothing illustrates so well the different patterns of life for men and women as the response of men to the day-time courses. Only a handful joined them during the eight years under review. They included two retired men, three men with their own small businesses, two taxi-drivers, a driving instructor, a night porter, a night telephone operator, a security guard, and several men able to do part-time or casual work according to their own wishes. Half of them substantially completed their courses, the extent to which they did so depending largely on the strength of their ultimate aim but dictated somewhat by the vagaries of their employment. But, in the face of what some of them felt to be a monstrous regiment of better educated women dominating the class (although these were always friendly and helpful), men without a strong motivation or considerable self-confidence tended to drop out. Shift-workers who did survive included the security guard, the hotel porter, the night telephone operator, and the two taxi-drivers. One of them went to a university, one to a college of education and one to a long-term residential college. Among the other stickers were the owner of a private hotel who went on to study with the Open University and a young man who was preparing himself to enter a family business.

What the day courses did provide were opportunities for serious educational effort by the occasional man who, for whatever personal or occupational reasons, happened to be free in the day-time or could stand the rigours of combining night work and study and the challenge of a predominantly female group. One example will be illustrative:

S.T. Born 1946. Aged 27 at start of course in 1973; single. Working as international telephonist GPO and adjusted shift working to attend the course. Had previously done a variety of jobs including a year as a lighthouse keeper. Left a comprehensive school at 16 with four 'O's and two RSAs. Joined the course to broaden scope of study while working on his own for 'A' level history as a requirement for taking history as his preferred main subject at a college of education. Passed 'A' level and went to the college of his choice. Says the Fresh Horizons course 'helped me to appreciate and enjoy my present course of study more than I would have, I am sure, without its assistance. In particular it has given me self-confidence and broadened my scope of reading.'

Part-time day courses might draw more men in times and areas of unemployment, but where there are full employment possibilities, there is a real danger of reinforcing the existing difficulties and feelings of inadequacy of a man who already has problems of reconciling himself to the demands of our society. This applies with less force to the full-time day courses where students are recognized as qualifying for maintenance grants and are on a more equal footing with the women.

4
Evening students and some comparisons

Although historically associated with the City of London, the City Lit is, in fact, outside its boundaries, lying just off the route from the East to the West End of London where Drury Lane starts its course down towards the Strand. It draws its evening students from the City's commercial houses, the nearby law centres and publishing and insurance businesses and the retail trade beyond Seven Dials. All these enterprises make an especial demand for the services of young women offering new annual sacrifices to Minos via the typist's chair and the filing cabinet.

Lying beyond the commercial centres is a hinterland of bed-sitters and shared flats to which the office staffs return at nights. The City Lit, although obscurely placed, is a convenient call on the way home from work, for refreshment of the body at the canteen or coffee bar and the satisfaction of the mind in cultural and intellectual ways. The City Lit staff were aware how much this was part of a pattern of life for several thousand young people, particularly young women. The evening population was markedly different from the day-time one, but it was a fair assumption that an adaptation of the Fresh Horizons course could provide a basis for new educational and vocational possibilities for some who might otherwise feel that they had reached the end of the road they had trodden from school. By arranging for a double period on two evenings a week from 6 to 9.15 p.m. (including a coffee break) it was possible to make a six-hour part-time course of four subjects that would only lose the mathematics and tutorial period of the day-time one. The mathematics could be offered later in the year as an individual subject and tutorial and counselling hours were fixed, not wholly conveniently because of the tightness of the schedule, for two hours each evening of the course from 4.45 to 6.45 p.m., thereby slightly overlapping the teaching periods.

Women on the evening courses

A few examples will indicate the characteristics of the women, their reasons for seeking to enrol and the resulting outcomes.

A.C. Born 1919. Aged 49 at the time of the course in 1968. Single. Lived with mother. Bank clerk for twenty-nine years but fearing redundancy or loss of status from mergers. Left elementary school at 14, having moved from a private grammar school during the 1930s depression. Learnt shorthand at evening classes and had also taken classes in first aid, cookery, woodwork and German. Had been a special constable and was in the Civil Nursing Reserve. After the Fresh Horizons course took a special entry test and was accepted for training at a college of education.

She wrote later 'I have now been teaching almost five years. It's a hard and tiring profession but I love it.'

B.D. Born 1932. Aged 37 at the time of the course in 1969. Single. Senior secretary. Left grammar school at 16 with matric exemption in the school certificate examination. Says family circumstances did not permit training for social work or teaching to both of which she was attracted. Was active over the years as a voluntary church worker and club leader and did and organized many part-time courses for this, but realized that changes in her job and the approach of 40 made her vulnerable. After the course, with considerable difficulty and applications to every social work course in the country, secured a place on a two-year full-time course for a Certificate in Social Work which she passed well. Wrote subsequently 'I'm very happily settled with a new job, new flat, new car in a New Town.'

C.E. Born 1944. Aged 25 at start of course in 1969. Single. Clerical worker BBC. Left independent school at 16 with eight 'O's. Did three 'A's in a year at a crammers but did not get into university of choice so did secretarial subjects. Had short spells in Italy for language study. After the Fresh Horizons course studied full-time for a London external degree at a polytechnic and obtained a 2 (1) Honours. Followed this with a one-year teaching diploma course and now teaches at a college of further education.

D.F. Born 1943. Aged 27 when she joined the course in 1970. Married with two children aged 3 and 5. Formerly a tracer in a drawing office. Left a secondary modern school at 16 with one 'O' level and RSA's in English, arithmetic and technical drawing. Had passed the 11-plus but 'parents wouldn't let me attend the school as it was too far away and they didn't bother to try for a more convenient alternative. Basically my parents thought education was a waste of time, particularly for girls. They never showed any interest (attending open days, etc.). My school reports were never read. I was never encouraged and being a lazy child I just didn't work. After school went to evening classes in dressmaking and guitar-playing. I was very bogged down into trying to fit myself into the woman's magazine ideal mum image. I have now realized it is much easier to be me and I honestly believe my family benefits from it.' After Fresh Horizons course started studying with the Open University.

E.G. Born 1920. Aged 52 at start of course in 1972. Was suffering effects of marriage break-up. Had one son at university. Left school, elementary, before fourteenth birthday. Says 'At the age of 8 I contracted a kidney disease which kept me away from school for five months and somehow I never seemed to catch up. From then on most of school was pretty nightmarish.' Went to work as a welder in an aircraft factory for two years then as a telephonist on and off for thirty. Has since worked in hospitals and social service departments as a receptionist. Hoped to be accepted as a welfare assistant but the chance has been reduced by economy cuts. Over the years has had extensive involvement as an actress with good amateur companies. To boost self-confidence took 'O' level English after finishing Fresh Horizons course and with minimum preparation got an 'A' grade. Is an active supporter of the Fresh Horizons club and is a member of City Lit drama groups. Reads books on to tape for the National Listening Library.

H.J. Born 1947. Aged 25 at start of course in 1972. Single. Fairly casual work in shops, offices and as a nursery helper. Went to secondary modern school but did not go back after hospitalization for rheumatic fever, age 14. Says 'I regarded my illness as a gift from God as I couldn't bear my school anyway and was continually playing truant.' Saw possibilities in education when working as typist for American college summer schools in England. Attended some art classes at the City Lit before joining Fresh Horizons course and then at tutor's suggestion went on to the first full-time course. Accepted as a mature entrant without formal qualifications for university a year later.

The difference in age between the mostly married women of the day courses and the mainly single women of the evening ones was emphasized in Table 2. Taking the whole group of 142 who joined the evening courses, nearly half were under 30 years of age, three-quarters under 40; three-quarters of the day students were between 30 and 50. Of the women evening students 80 per cent were either single (65 per cent) or widowed, divorced or separated (15 per cent). Only a few of the remaining 20 per cent of married students still had children at home.

The evening-course students drawn from this different population were therefore no longer mainly housewives, frustrated because they had worked through their span of total domestic involvement.

Table 7 *Registered students and questionnaire respondents—comparison of marital status*

	women				men	
	day			evening	day	evening
	1966–9	1970–3	Total	1968–73	1966–73	1968–73
registered N =	77	91	168	142	20	58
	%	%	%	%	(N)	%
married	75	71	73	20	(7)	29
single	9	13	11	65	(11)	57
married formerly	16	16	16	15	(2)	14
questionnaire respondents N =	49	56	105	53	9	27
	%	%	%	%	(N)	(N)
married	80	68	74	19	(4)	(7)
single	8	11	9	64	(4)	(14)
married formerly	12	21	17	17	(1)	(6)

They were largely single, clerical workers. Still young, they were well past the end of their commercial apprenticeship; they were experienced in the ways of commerce and administration but their entry into responsible management was estopped by traditional business mores. It was still an essentially female population: the reasons for this were presented more fully in Chapter 2 but there are immediately obvious reasons why such an outcome was probable. The preponderance of office jobs in the catchment area, with a consequent large intake of girls from the suburbs and provinces, and the attraction to women of a liberal arts programme as offered by the City Lit were good reasons why women joining the evening Fresh Horizons courses outnumbered men by more than two to one.

It was also a determinant of the occupational level of the students, 80 per cent of whom were classifiable as 'junior non-manual' and 13 per cent as 'intermediate non-manual'. Only a few, over the years, had something approaching more advanced professional or managerial status.

Some 38 per cent were the product, educationally, of publicly provided grammar schools. With the addition of those from private day and boarding schools, the proportion with assumed superior schooling was about two-thirds. The remainder finished childhood education at elementary or secondary modern schools.

Fifty-three of them, who for the most part were representative of the whole, completed the questionnaires that were distributed to all reasonably regular attenders. Of these, nineteen left school at 15 or under, fifteen at 16 years of age and nineteen at 17 or over. More than a third, therefore, had left school at what was, for their time, the minimum school-leaving age, but two-thirds had stayed to or beyond the higher minimum of today. The percentage details are given earlier in Table 3.

The school-leaving qualifications of this and other groups are shown in Table 8.

Twenty-nine of the evening respondents felt that their early education had been adversely affected by social, family and personal hazards. For this group, war and evacuation were equalled by the vagaries of the 11-plus and childhood illness as claimed causes of schooling loss. But many of them who had 'A' levels or five or more 'O' levels in GCE examinations had left school with further potential unexplored, having had as much in the way of

Table 8 *Respondents—qualification levels on basis of public examinations at school*

qualification levels	women day 1966–9	women day 1970–3	women Total	women evening 1968–73	men day 1966–73	men evening 1968–73
N =	49	56	105	53	7	27
6	4	9	13	6	–	6
7	14	14	28	17	1	1
6 & 7 (%)	(37%)	(41%)	(39%)	(43%)	–	(26%)
8	4	5	9	5	1	1
9	3	1	4	–	1	1
10	2	2	4	3	–	1
11	1	–	1	1	–	1
6–11 (%)	(57%)	(55%)	(56%)	(60%)	–	(41%)
approx. national equivalent per General Household Survey 1973, Table 7.14				(18%)		(26%)

Key:

6 = 1 or more GCE 'A'/HSC and/or City and Guilds Advanced Final and/or ONC/OND.

7 = 5 or more GCE 'O'/CSE Grade 1 and/or City and Guilds Craft Ordinary.

8 = 1–4 'O' levels GCE or CSE Grade 1 with clerical/commercial qualifications.

9 = as 8 without clerical/commercial qualifications.

10 = clerical and commercial qualifications only.

11 = CSE lower and unknown grades.

(NB: equivalent Scottish qualifications are included as appropriate.)

education as they, their parents or their mentors had thought was sufficient 'for a girl'.

Thirty out of fifty-three recorded education or training after leaving school (in sixteen instances, full-time) leading to a certificate, for the most part concerned with immediate employment. These were mainly girls who had taken full-time office-skill courses of various lengths, but there were a few who, with two- or three-year courses in design, domestic science or medical auxiliary training behind them, were bent on building up to graduate level or escaping into a new career. For the rest, post-school education for work meant evening classes in shorthand and typing. All but a few, over the years, had done their evening stints of drama, art, languages, physical recreation and humanities subjects at the City Lit and elsewhere. What were they now looking for outside their jobs and over and beyond these spare-time cultural activities?

Motivations and outcomes

Students were asked 'What prompted you to apply?' The description of the course in the prospectus suggested it could have a vocational appeal as pre-professional study or be helpful as a preparation for higher education, but it also emphasized its value for intellectual development in its own right. An analysis of the replies to this question is given separately for respondents from the day and evening courses respectively in Table 9.

It is apparent that women on the day courses were much more tentative in claiming a vocational motive—only one in six mentioned a specific intent—but there was frequently a submerged one: 'To get me out of the home', 'To gain confidence to study further', 'A need for a new orientation'. But the main emphasis was on the need for mental stimulus—'To widen my interests', 'A need to fill up the gaps', and to emerge from the loneliness of a purely domestic life, 'General unrest after twenty years of domestication', 'Loneliness after my youngest child started school'. They also liked the nature of the course—'Needed more than the usual course', 'No exams', 'Wanted a day course in several subjects', 'The name describes it'.

Among these women there was a need to build up confidence in their ability to confront a different world from that of home, family and neighbours, to try themselves out in a small pond before launching themselves on to a larger sea.

The timing of the course mattered more to them than it did to the evening students: it had to fit in with the domestic pattern of minutiae of duties, children to be convoyed, husbands to be placated and social obligations fulfilled. Time on their hands was broken up by the scheduled and unscheduled calls of domestic life, and although in taking the course they were experimenting with new patterns, the old were still paramount.

Table 9   *Respondents—stated reasons for joining courses*

	women		men
	day	evening	evening
analysis of stated motives	all years	all years	all years
N =	105	53	27
vocational			
higher education	4	7	4
teaching	7	8	2
social work	1	3	1
job related	5	10	7
number of students	17	28	14
non-vocational			
general	33	10	2
exploratory	1	3	4
return to study	42	23	10
nature of course			
timing	19	2	3
'serious'	6	5	1
number of stated motives (multiple)	101	43	20

Additional questions were asked in the hope of making a more realistic assessment of underlying motives for joining: were they, in the main, related to preparing for further education or training for new or different work or to extending their own development in a more general way? If the former, had they a specific aim in mind? Had they changed their mind on this during the course and if so in what direction—from the former to the latter or vice versa? It is worth looking at the responses to these questions by both day and evening students in relation to four areas of outcome, i.e. commitment to conventional university degree courses, teacher training, social work training or Open University study. Figures for day and evening students are given separately in Table 10. (These overlap with, but differ from, the figures in Table 9 because they derive from answers to different questions.)

Table 10 *Respondents (women) on day and evening courses—intentions and outcomes regarding higher education*

	numbers		
women on day courses (N = 105)	original aim	not defined as aim	outcome
type of higher education			
degree—conventional	–	10	10
Open University	–	5	5
teacher training	8	12	20
social work training	3	2	5
women on evening courses (N = 53)			
type of higher education			
degree—conventional	4	4	8
Open University	2	6	8
teacher training	5	3	8
social work training	2	1	3

Of the ten day-time students who went on to take university degree courses, none intended to do so in the first place, but seven of them had some thought of entering work, further education or training. Some of them found an unsuspected academic bent in following their Fresh Horizons studies, others became aware that they could set their sights higher than they had thought. Teacher training was perhaps the most obvious developmental step for many of these students, but of the twenty-one who actually took that direction, only eight started with it as a defined intention.

Yet despite this process of self-discovery, there remained limits to the areas to which ambition could be directed. Commercial life offered little more to the better-prepared woman than it did to the raw commercial school-leaver. Many caring and paramedical professions were establishing entry requirements to attract sixth-form leavers and graduates that would mean several more years of preparation for adults educated to the limits of an earlier date. More part-time courses at all levels would have helped more people to phase out their old roles while assuming the new. For many of the students there had to be compromise between what they might have wished to do and what was possible or practicable.

For others the period of self-exploration afforded by the course helped in making decisions not to disturb the status quo but to settle for what they saw on the immediate horizon, sometimes to defer a decision until children were older or not to challenge domestic harmony too much. Very frequently students whose appetites had been whetted by the free yet demanding nature of the course they had just completed asked for a 'graduate' Fresh Horizons course, but resources were not available. Having learned something of how to tackle learning, some of them went on to build up 'A' levels or sought out more sophisticated non-certificate or University Extension diploma courses, often expressing satisfaction that they were now prepared to read a little more deeply, think a little more clearly and understand better the world around them.

In contrast to the day groups, over half the women on the evening courses claimed a vocational motive for joining from the outset. Many of them, however, expressed it in terms of dissatisfaction with an existing job rather than as a positive leaning towards one of the few professions that might be open to them. Boredom for them was boredom at work, the sameness of the shorthand-typist's job in whatever milieu they found themselves in the search for a more challenging working environment. The need to return to study, to rebuild confidence in learning skills was emphasized— 'After ten years, the very thing I needed', 'Keen to know if I could cope', 'A desire to learn to boost my morale', 'A need for mental stimulus'. The nature of the course was also mentioned—'The wish for a more disciplined course than the normal ones', 'Would help me more than an 'A' level course', 'It seemed to imply a comprehensive range of subjects in a complete course', 'The title fitted in with what I felt the need of', 'The wording in the prospectus seemed to have been written just for me'.

But many came intending to take the opportunity to change to teaching or to another form of higher education—to take, ten or more years after leaving school, the course they might have taken had circumstances been different at the time. Even so there was a tendency for sights to be set lower than abilities warranted and more were encouraged to venture on university courses than had originally intended to do so, as the figures in Table 10 confirm.

The delight of the women students, both day and evening, who made their way into higher education was expressed in comments that often accompanied the returned questionnaires and in unbidden progress reports that arrived from time to time. The following extracts convey the flavour of these voluntary testimonies. (The ages given are those at the time of the Fresh Horizons course.)

'The Fresh Horizons course gave me tremendous confidence so that I dared to attempt the London School of Economics Diploma and try for an academic life. I can't divide the Fresh Horizons course from my new career as it was the beginning of a whole new way of life.'

(single woman: 43: formerly actress and secretary)

'Before attending the Fresh Horizons course I hadn't the faintest idea that it was possible for someone like myself with no qualifications even to apply for teacher training.'

(widow: 40: formerly nurse)

'I shall be eternally grateful to you for suggesting teacher training. I loved my three years at college and truly love being in school at last. I have more confidence in myself after achieving examination success in my forties and I'm told I'm more pleasant to be with at home than I was before Fresh Horizons.'

(married woman: 40: no previous career outside the home)

'Completely changed my life. Very happy doing a degree course. Only wish I had known twenty years ago that I was capable of this study.'

(married woman: two children: 39: formerly nurse)

'Filling in the questionnaire reminded me how incredibly lucky I was to stumble on Fresh Horizons. I am so grateful for all the help and encouragement I had.'

(married woman: three children: 31: housewife: formerly dental receptionist: on second year of degree course)

'Again I must say how glad I am for the Fresh Horizons course and the opportunity it has given me to work like this. Sometimes I wonder if I can make it but I suddenly realized I am enjoying it even if it does seem to be too much for me.'

(divorced woman: three children: 40: formerly shorthand-typist: on second year of degree course)

Men at night

Over the six years men formed less than one-third of the students on the evening courses. The age-group most strongly represented was from 30 to 39 (42 per cent). The under-30s, although less dominant than among the women, were a substantial 37 per cent. A much greater proportion of them were single than would be expected from national statistics. They came from a wider range of occupations and social backgrounds than the women, as is apparent from the following examples and from the figures in Table 11.

J.L. Born 1927. Aged 42 at time of course in 1969. Single, bank messenger. Formerly warehouseman, machine operator, driver, postal worker, national serviceman. Left school at 14 in 1941 and says, 'Schooling was limited during wartime. I've given this a lot of thought and realized my education finished at about eleven years of age.' Hampered by a stammer, a problem which he had already tackled before joining the Fresh Horizons course, having recently attended evening classes in public speaking, elocution and drama. Had done voluntary youth work, particularly as a physical training instructor at various times, which possibly helped him to obtain a place at a college of education where he studied (main subject English and Drama) for three years. Now teaches a multi-racial class in a junior school and speech in an adult institute.

K.M. Born 1942. Aged 27 at time of course in 1969. Single. Son of illiterate peasants who had fled from Spain into southern France during the civil war. Left elementary school in France at 14 and went through a bakery apprenticeship. Worked as a baker in France and in England where he came in 1967, having heard, as a member of a 'mutual improvement' society in France, of the opportunities for adult education at the long-term residential colleges. Went to Fircroft College after the Fresh Horizons course and from there obtained entry to university taking a third-class honours degree.

I.K. Born 1947. Aged 25 at time of course in 1972. Married with two children. Working as electrical systems faultfinder. Left secondary modern school at 15 without school-leaving qualifications and did five-year apprenticeship in electrical engineering. Attended technical college on day-release and passed qualifying City and Guilds certificates. Did voluntary work in youth club and attended special level classes in photography in spare time. Took two 'O' levels by correspondence while on part-time Fresh Horizons course and then went on to the first full-time course. Had strong interests in History of Art and Drama. Entered local university, 1973, to read for B.Sc. in Social Science, obtained an Upper Second and was accepted for postgraduate study.

L.N. Born 1945. Aged 27 at time of course in 1972. Married, no children. Police officer from leaving grammar school at 19 with five 'O's and one 'A' level. Interested in children's welfare and worked as volunteer in spare time. Decided, when on the course, to work for an Open University degree as most compatible with his job. Says Fresh Horizons course gave him a greater awareness of a need for objectivity at work.

M.O. Born 1941. Aged 30 at time of course in 1971. Single. Working as bus driver and was formerly a conductor. Went to various public authority boarding schools because of family difficulties. Left at 15 with no qualifications. Had attended public speaking classes at an ILEA adult evening institute, winning LAMDA medals. A friend there told him about the Fresh Horizons course at which he worked very hard in spite of shift duties. Says 'I learned more in weeks than I had hitherto in months.' Passed special entry test and entered a college of education.

Occupations represented included hospital clerk, jeweller, warehouseman, radio shop manager, insurance clerk, baker, production manager, solicitor, bus driver, bank messenger, computer techni-

Table 11 *Evening students—socio-occupational status by sex*

	women	men
totals enrolled 1968–73	142	58
in gainful employment	130	52
classification	%	%
prof/managerial	4	6
inter. non-manual	13	25
junior non-manual	80	38
skilled manual	–	10
partly-skilled manual	2	19
unskilled manual	1	2

cian, civil servants of various grades, clerical and office supervisory workers in variety.

This summary analysis will sufficiently indicate the wide spread of basic educational equipment these men brought to the courses. In formal terms it ranged from a foreign-born degree-level professional man, through a small group with 'A' levels (including several public-school boys disappointed in their post-school expectations and several with foreign equivalents), some with 'O' levels or technician qualifications, to others without a certificate to their names. All-in-all they represented a formidable variety of early educational experience. They were much more likely than the women to have completed schooling at secondary modern, central or technical schools. This connects with the fact that of the twenty-seven who completed questionnaires, two-thirds had left school at 15 or under and three-quarters had left at or below today's minimum leaving age as shown in Table 3. They therefore represent something much nearer to the national average of educational background and underline the extent to which men, in our society, are raised to higher level jobs and women are submerged in lower level ones, than their respective educational preparations would seem to warrant.

This is not to deny the miscasting of boys and men, by the vagaries of our educational arrangements or the chances of time and circumstances, in less prestigious roles than their capacities would justify. More of the male evening students than of the female claimed disturbance of their early education by physical or social causes. These included war-time disturbances both at home and abroad, but also 11-plus hazards, parental separation and inadequacies of career counselling at school. The value of the course, if only as a retrieval agent, is demonstrated by what it enabled some of them to achieve. Five who subsequently went on to degree courses and three who went to colleges of education all came from secondary modern or equivalent schools and only one of them had stayed at school as late as 16 years of age. Only two had obtained qualifying certificates, and those minor ones, at school. Most of those going on had already found their way into adult education and indeed this goes for the whole group of respondents, nineteen out of the twenty-seven of whom recorded previous contact with classes in art, music, languages, speech, psychology or with correspondence study for GCE examinations. What the Fresh Horizons

Table 12 *Respondents (men) on evening courses—subsequent educational commitments*

type of course	numbers pursuing
degree—conventional	9
college of education	3
training—new work	2
Open University	2
adult residential college	1
'A' levels GCE	2
non-certificate adult education	4
not recorded	4
	27

course did for many of them was to challenge peremptorily the low estimation put on their capacities at school and build on the confidence they had gradually been establishing through classes related to hobbies, leisure interests and their search for self-improvement. Table 12 summarizes the educational follow-up by these men of their Fresh Horizons courses.

Comments on their aims and satisfactions, recorded by some of these students, show the individual nature of the responses to the course and their outcomes.

'. . . as a student my college studies are my foremost interest and occupy most of my time. Thanks to Fresh Horizons my whole concept of education has broadened and become intense and absorbing . . . the whole course gave me a great new confidence.'
(college of education student, aged 44, formerly bank messenger)

'I have a much greater awareness of what I want to do and how to go about doing it.'
(Former draughtsman and guitar player—taking BA in music)

'The drama was a great help—very important. Without laying it on, I thoroughly enjoyed the course—quite frankly it was the determining factor that led me to a change of vocation.'
(Manager of complaints department in a hardware store and spare-time entertainer who became 'artist-director of a variety agency')

'Two main reasons stopped me pursuing further courses. First, we had to move into more spacious accommodation. Secondly, we have since had another child. Although I have not pursued any specific further education since the course, I will be forever grateful that I became involved with it. My wife and closest friends noticed the beneficial effect on me.'

(Newspaper van-driver who had to give up intention of going to a residential college)

and a comment on the decision-making process:

'I had an idea to apply for a course leading to an "A" level or maybe Open University—also an intention not clearly defined to aim for a degree course in English but changed my mind during the Fresh Horizons course. I became more convinced that I didn't want a degree course but to write. I have been directed away from institutional education and into pursuing my own educational interests. For the moment, I will add, since I am again contemplating a degree course.'

(Former merchant seaman who left the sea after getting his second-mate's ticket and took part-time clerical work with the aim of becoming a writer)

Open University students—a comparison

As an addendum to this account of Fresh Horizons students it is possible, from information now made available about the first year's intake of Open University students, to make some comparisons between the people caught in a large national net and the Fresh Horizons students of the same period. Some people actually enrolled for Fresh Horizons courses as a deliberate preparation for Open University study or with the possibility in mind, after testing their ability to tackle serious and demanding study. But in the upshot, the number of Fresh Horizons students who finally decided to study with the Open University was not large.

There is a close resemblance in the age-groups attracted.[1] The dominant group in all cases falls within the range 25 to 44, with more Open University students near the lower half of the range as compared with the somewhat older part-time day and younger part-time evening Fresh Horizons students. There are similarities in other age-groups except for men in the years between 45 and 54 and there are too few men in the Fresh Horizons group for much importance to attach to this. Educationally, there is some resemblance between the proportions of the women students who had grammar and grammar-type schooling, 76 per cent in the case of Open University students compared with about 68 per cent of Fresh Horizons students, but Fresh Horizons men at 34 per cent compare with 67 per cent of Open University men.[2] The considerable number of teachers among the Open University students suggests a greater proportion of them as having school-leaving qualifications and post-school full-time education. Proportionately more Fresh Horizons students left school prematurely, either leaving grammar school without 'O' levels, or having rejected the chance to take 'A' levels, and in this they were probably more typical of their generation's grammar-school output than were the first batch of Open University students.

Although exact comparisons are difficult, there is considerable agreement in the reporting of disadvantages experienced during early education. Of Open University students who volunteered information 28 per cent referred to war and evacuation;[3] 25 per cent of the women respondents from the day Fresh Horizons courses said the same. Family removals with consequent frequent changes of school and childhood illness, were important factors in reducing the effectiveness of early education for members of both groups.

The Open University study reinforces the evidence from the Fresh Horizons courses that the life-long effects of social disruption and change, including those within the educational system itself, as well as individual life hazards, should be given much greater weight than they now are in educational policies and planning, whether inside or beyond formal schooling. People who embark on education in mature life will always be subject to unavoidable pressures and constraints that must be recognized and eased as far as possible in policy-making and conduct of courses.

5
A full-time course

No doubt the clear success of the part-time courses, and recognition of similarities with the work of the one- and two-year courses offered by the residential colleges for adults, helped to shape the thoughts of the policy-makers in the direction of this distinct innovation. The crucial point, of course, was the implication that the Inner London Education Authority would be prepared to make discretionary grants to cover student maintenance and the suggested tuition fee of £50, which was effectively a vote of confidence in the whole Fresh Horizons enterprise.

It had, nevertheless, to conform to the pattern of full-time courses already established within the authority's range of further-education establishments, whose students were eligible for similar grant-aid. This meant attendance by students for twenty hours a week for teaching and tutorial purposes and an approved programme of subjects and classes extending over thirty weeks. A recruitment of twenty-four students was envisaged, and two full-time tutors, with help from part-time staff, were to be responsible both for the new full-time students and for the part-time courses that were to continue as an essential part of the whole programme. The full-time staff would also provide a counselling service for Fresh Horizons and other City Lit students as well as for members of the general public.

Subjects

The core subjects proposed that are discussed more fully in the next chapter were those that had already proved themselves of value to students on the part-time courses. They were to be regarded as starting points for exploration rather than as elements of formal study: the point was strongly made at the time that, although seemingly subject-directed, the course was devised to allow for maximum inter-relation between the different elements. The prospectus presented these concepts in the following way:

> The basic subjects are chosen to provide foundation studies in a number of aspects of human culture. The intention is that while extending the range of their knowledge students will develop skills of expression and learning.
>
> No objective standard is set. The course aims to start where the individual student is and to lead as far as the student is willing and able to go. Students' work will be continuously assessed and recommendations will be on the quality and standard achieved.
>
> The course subjects are approached in a varied and informal way including study groups and seminars as well as lectures and discussions and are as follows:
>
> *English, Spoken and Written* comprising practice in the use of good English as a tool in writing, thought and argument, the appreciation of style and the development of powers of creative writing.
>
> *English Literature*   The course includes the study of the novel, poetry and drama for aesthetic enjoyment and the enlargement of the understanding.
>
> *Social Studies* in which are considered aspects of society relating to its structure, history, activities and the social theories of philosophers and others.
>
> *A New Approach to Mathematics*   The aim is to introduce the ideas and concepts of mathematics today and some of the basic language and to examine how mathematics can influence our ways of thinking.
>
> *Tutorials*   The tutor meets an individual student or a small group for examination and discussion of a subject, thus enabling personal study difficulties to be more easily settled.

These core elements were designed to absorb fourteen hours of the twenty. The remaining six hours were available for optional subjects chosen, after consultation with the tutor, from the large number of alternatives provided by the City Lit's general programme in the fields of humanities, foreign languages, art, music and drama. Optional subjects could be taken outside the normal course hours of 10.30–5.00 and the course was concentrated in four days a week to help housewives, to give all students a chance of more concentrated home study time and to allow for the evening hours worked by tutors. The study programme included two residential weekend courses on themes related to the main course.

Recruitment

The tutor-organizer moved from part-time to full-time duties in May 1973 and set publicity in motion. Apart from a small poster produced by the media resources officer of the City Lit and sent to all main and branch libraries within the catchment area, the only other cash outlay for publicity was on postage. Letters to interested organizations, a press release with approaches to journalistic sympathizers in press and radio to give it a mention—these, together with internal City Lit publicity, all produced applicants directly or indirectly. Some of the applicants were helped to consider more appropriate outlets for their ambitions, but the course opened in September with twenty-three students and two more were added later.

In the main, students were selected on the basis of their lack of formal academic qualifications: only one, a housewife, had anything like university entry qualifications—a quarter-of-a-century-old higher school certificate. Applicants were not asked to supply written work other than a statement of between three and five hundred words on why they wanted to do the course. This was taking more of a chance than the residential colleges have usually been willing to take but a demand for presentation of an essay, even with a wide choice of themes, was likely to daunt otherwise suitable applicants. A personal statement presented problems for some, but at least it concerned a subject on which the applicants were all 'experts'; while helping them to clarify their aims it demonstrated the extent of their powers of literate expression to the interviewers.

The recruits

The oldest of the twenty-five enrolled students was 44, the youngest, 22. As with the part-time courses, there was a heavy predominance of women, as is clear from Table 13.

Table 13   *Marital status, age and sex of full-time students, 1973–4*

students	marital status			numbers in age-groups				
	S	M	MF	–24	25–29	30–34	35–39	40–44
women	12	5	5	5	5	4	5	3
men	2	1	–	–	2	–	–	1
total	14	6	5	5	7	4	5	4

S = single   M = married   MF = married formerly

The first full-time women students were similar in age to part-time evening students of the same sex, with nearly half of them under 30 and almost two-thirds of them under 35 in both cases. Similarly, in both groups the response came predominantly from single women including women married formerly. They differed sharply in this from the women on the part-time day courses of whom 74 per cent were currently married. All the full-time women students who were formerly or currently married had children at home but they were less than half the total enrolled. This difference in response to the full-time as opposed to the part-time day courses, serves to emphasize the difficulties that women with children experience in committing themselves to full-time courses with substantial attendance requirements. Those who joined the full-time course were, in fact, as regular in attendance as any of the other students, but replies to questionnaires showed consciousness of more domestic pressures related both to housework and to family care.

When the full-time course was mooted, fears were expressed in the education department at County Hall that it would be seized upon overwhelmingly by rather dilettante middle-class and middle-aged women seeking predigested culture. This was a curious fear since such women had been little in evidence among part-time day students, and the demanding nature of the proposed full-time course was likely to be a powerful deterrent to anyone without a serious commitment. Similar fears, that proved equally groundless, were that the course would prove particularly attractive to male students from overseas. In fact they were much more likely to be looking for courses with hard-and-fast exit qualifications.

The occupational experience of the full-time women students

was very similar to that of women on the part-time courses. Over four-fifths of them had been in work classed as junior non-manual and only two of them had been in work that could be regarded as implying greater responsibilities. Yet eight had taken full-time courses straight from school, largely in commercial subjects, and might have been regarded as qualified for promotion were it not for their sex. One single woman of 28 summed up the position when she wrote in her application, 'Having worked for just over eight years in the world of commerce, I find that scope for me is limited and does not provide my mind with any stimulation.'

The sharpest difference between the full-time and part-time women students was in their early education. Just under two-thirds of the former left school before they were 16, half of this group having left at under 15, even though for some of them this had already become the statutory leaving age. Reasons given for this included illness, administrative concessions about leaving dates and, to some extent 'school refusal'. In later accounts of their schooldays, two of the fourteen early leavers admitted to regular truancy. By contrast, only one-third of the women attending part-time had left school at 15 or under and, correspondingly, more of them had school-leaving qualifications of some kind—more than half of them as against less than a quarter of the full-time students.

It would be misleading to try to generalize from the characteristics and experience of the three men who were enrolled for the first full-time course. They resembled the men enrolled at Fircroft College, who are considered in Chapter 11, and the men on the part-time evening Fresh Horizons courses, in that they were all school-leavers at 15 and came from similar occupational levels. Two were single, one was a young married man with a family. They had no school-leaving qualifications, but the two younger men had acquired an 'O' level or so after leaving school.

It can be added that men with similar defining characteristics were a markedly larger proportion of those accepted for the full-time course in subsequent years.

Educational lag

With this kind of recruitment of full-time students, the Fresh Horizons offer was disturbing another layer of educational lag. The relegation (as most of them felt it) to the secondary modern school, on the results of an 11-plus test, was one aspect. 'I felt a failure' wrote one and another recorded, more extensively, 'Going to a secondary modern school, in my parents' view, excluded me from getting a worth-while job. I gave up before I started; I played truant very frequently at the secondary modern school till I was fourteen. My last two years at a comp. were more fruitful but I was refused a place in the GCE class on grounds of not being bright enough.' This girl was subsequently offered places at two universities and a polytechnic to read for a combined English and Italian degree, having learnt Italian as an *au pair*.

The resulting exclusions from qualifying examinations, modified by the introduction of the CSE [1] too late for most of them, left such students with a lack of an objective in their school lives and with feelings of inferiority that remained with them until they could prove themselves anew on the Fresh Horizons course. The demand for clerical labour, however, gave them an entry, via shorthand-typing, into a buoyant job-market that contributed something to their self-esteem. Experience of a rising standard of living, and the easy contacts made at home and abroad within the freedom of the youth culture, gave incentives to further self-development to the intelligent younger women that encouraged them to seize the chance afforded by the full-time Fresh Horizons course. For some of these early leavers at least, part-time study opportunities presented too many problems of discipline and organization of time and effort that could not easily be overcome. They were lively minded but restless as full-time students, easily aroused but easily daunted.

But not all the early leavers belonged to this group. A few older women had experienced educational loss through family poverty, war-time disruption or the uneven geographical spread of educational opportunity, misfortunes shared with many of the part-time students.

Surveying the entrants to this first full-time course, as a whole, illustrates and confirms that for a variety of reasons, personal, family, social and economic or, by reason of the vagaries of educational theory and administrative practice, there will continue to be a need for formally offered recurrent education. It will need to be provided in varied ways, full-time and part-time, to enable people to compensate for earlier loss, to keep abreast of rising standards or to satisfy urges to achieve better understanding of themselves and the world around them, whenever and however such urges are released.

Commitment

The first group of full-time students, with their marked differences of age, early education and ways of life, offered a continual challenge to the tutors. They were alive to ideas, they could counter reported facts with personal observation and experience, but tutors could not assume a comfortable background of school-derived academic competence at a given level. Gaps in general knowledge and vocabulary had to be filled in during the ceaseless questioning of fundamental concepts that accompanied any collective study period. The more knowledgeable students had to learn to bear with the less but their interests had also to be borne in mind. Classroom work was more intense and more intensive than in the part-time courses. Full-time students had a commitment in time and money that allowed little room for escape. Even the least conscientious were made continually aware of the pressure exerted on and by their fellow students. Tutorial and counselling sessions were searching and prolonged. The need to make decisions about the future, the cry of 'what comes after', the exploration of possibilities within themselves and in the world that lay before them, added their own tensions to the learning situation both for the students and the tutors. Yet there was also exhilaration in new enjoyments of reading and discussion, in the absorption of new concepts that shed light on previous experience and in the temporary total commitment to a way of life outside the 'getting and spending' of the workaday world.

By contrast, students often found the change of tempo in their optional studies deflating. If they could pursue an established interest, and classes were available at the right level (languages, drama, art, history, audio-visual communication and techniques were examples in the first year), they were happy in their choices and played fair by them. But some, caught up in their reading, essays and the close group of their own course associates, found insistence on six hours' attendance at optional classes irksome and resented this degree of direction of their activities. For others who, for example, needed to make a more concentrated attack on the use of English, extra tutorial time was substituted.

Assessment and outcomes

It was a basic element in the course planning that there would be no final examination or awards. Instead, in the last week of the session, each student presented to the whole group of students and tutorial staff an extended essay or a report on an individual project agreed with a tutor earlier in the course. Faced by intensive questioning and discussion from their audience, this was both a challenge to individual students and a pooling of information and experience for the whole group. It also contributed to making final assessments and reports although, long before this, tutors had to make interim assessments for purposes of entry to continued higher education. Admissions tutors in universities and polytechnics like neatly graded achievement levels, but the Fresh Horizons students were unknown quantities and were being recommended by unknowns. It says a good deal for the care with which assessments were compiled, for the capacities of the students to cope with interviews and for the willingness of some departmental heads to take chances, that the first year's full-time students received the welcome they did. The immediate outcome for the group of twenty-five was that eleven were accepted for degree courses at nearby polytechnics; five went on to degree courses at universities and two to certificate courses at colleges of education. Of the remainder, four returned to their work (one to a job at a considerably enhanced salary); two married women with families had to delay decisions because of uncertainties about places of residence; one single woman was seeking full-time work experience as a prelude to a possible social work career.

As with the part-time students, the knowledge that the course itself provided opportunities not previously known or seen as relevant created aspirations that needed careful sifting. Students were subject to the mounting pressure of the discussion of possible outcomes that became part of their environment. It is part of the environment of students of all ages at the point of passing from one stage to another, but the problems it raises are particularly acute for adults with livings to earn, families to care for and with an uncertain knowledge of their own capacities. There is a heavy investment in hope easily discounted by fear.

Outcomes compared

Compared to the full-time day students in the same year, the outcome for part-time students was markedly different. Continued study commitments for the group of evening students included two entrants without formal qualifications to universities; two who started Open University courses; two who entered the next year's full-time Fresh Horizons course; one who started the two-year course at Coleg Harlech; one who embarked on a social work training course and one who took a correspondence course for a civil service promotion examination, which she passed. The part-time day-time group included four prospective Open University students; one entrant to a college of education and one who followed up with the full-time Fresh Horizons course. But there were a number of others whose educational extension included courses for executive secretary, literacy tutor, London guide, extra-mural diploma and GCE 'A' and 'O' levels. Fewer people enrolled in the part-time courses with the clear intention of seeking full-time higher education; more were seeking educational experience as a basis for continuance of their own leisure-time studies or testing the feasibility of encouraging uncertain ambitions. And there were those who needed time to come to decisions about themselves, but in the meantime found a benefit that rubbed off on their children or their present job prospects. In this the part-time courses, more than the full-time ones, were gathering grounds for people with various needs.

Nevertheless, a larger proportion of part-time students, over the years, might have had more educational benefit if entry to degree courses, for which many of them had the intellectual capacity, had been easier, and if more part-time degree-level courses had been available. More flexibility in this way and transferability of credits between universities, polytechnics and the Open University would have opened new worlds to students who were compelled, by the actualities of their situations, to stifle nascent ambitions.

In the later years covered by this account, advanced courses within the reach of Fresh Horizons students, increased considerably. Polytechnics, more of them than of conventional universities territorially accessible, had extended their range of offerings into the humanities; the pressure for places from school-leavers had, to some extent, subsided; some institutions were becoming aware of the special contributions mature students had to offer. All these factors, coupled with the full-time availability for the first time, of the tutor organizer and another staff member, made approaches on behalf of students easier. For the full-time students there was evidence to offer of a full year's work, a reassurance to admissions tutors of steadiness of interest and purpose.

Mutual aid

The value of total immersion in an educational environment and the opportunities provided for student interaction have often been advanced to support claims for the importance of residential forms of adult as of other levels of education. It might be thought that mutual support could not be much in evidence when students assembled in the morning, dispersed in the afternoon and had the exclusive use of only one classroom during that time. But as it turned out, it was their 'den' for the time being. It was a part-time student who stressed how important it had been to her own group's identity to meet continuously in a particular room, but it was equally important for the full-timers that for the core of their studies they met as a group and were not dispersed on separate courses. Otherwise, on the physical plane, the City Lit, with its lounge areas, library, canteen and coffee-bar, allowed for plentiful informal contacts among students outside the hours of formal studies.

Despite these circumstances, more favourable than those often prevailing in adult education, it might still seem unlikely that a group of non-resident students, disparate in age and all of them having established circles of friends within reach of their homes, would achieve much in the way of student friendships and mutual support as important elements in the course. This, however, was not how the full-time students felt about it; those replying to the questionnaire were unanimous about the value they derived from each other's company and expressed themselves freely about it, e.g.

> 'We met for unofficial tutorials, play-readings and the like.'
> 'Great benefit . . . it was a delight to be able to talk to other interested people about the things that interested me. Other people's viewpoints also widened my understanding of the subject.'
> 'Yes, 100 per cent. I did not feel at all isolated fighting my own battle to break into the world of study.'

'Others were learning to study and we encouraged each other.'
'To realize one is but an individual among many such
attempting to pursue "lost time" in education is itself
comforting but to realize that the majority of those other
individuals shared so many problems was really an important
feature of the course.'
'We were able to exchange hopes and fears and many
problems which made me realize I was not alone and some
people had much worse problems than me. We became a sort
of "neurotics anonymous".' (A less terrifying thought than it
would be in a residential setting!)
'The contact with my fellow-students was of supreme value
and of as much educational value as the course itself. A large
part of the success of the course was what I can only describe
as class dynamics fostered and encouraged by the type of
course and the style of teaching.'

'Type of course' and 'style of teaching'—may it not be that for
the maximizing of mutual student aid, these are more important
than physical environments, residential or non-residential?

6
Contents of a package

The apparently arbitrary and authoritarian design of the courses as package deals to be accepted as a whole was contrary to the common post-war pattern of local authority adult education and to the tenor of much contemporary discussion about student choice and participation in decision-making. In pre-war days, further education craft-certificate courses, offered largely to adolescents in evening institutes—or night-schools as they were more commonly called—had followed prescribed syllabuses and made the study of a group of subjects compulsory. From the late 1940s, with the raising of the school-leaving age and an increase in day-release classes at the apprentice level, many of these courses, or their modernized equivalents, moved over into the lower-level colleges of further education.

The vacuum that would otherwise have been created was more than filled by an upsurge of demand from adults, although it was some time before the full import of this change was widely seized. Their preferences were mainly for the once-a-week pursuit of leisure-time interests, an emphasis officially encouraged by the Department of Education in Pamphlet No. 8, *Further Education*, issued in 1947. The limited pre-war provision of domestic-craft classes—woodwork, dressmaking and basic cookery—as all that was on offer by way of LEA provision for adults, blossomed into home decoration, creative embroidery, continental cookery and much fancily named physical activity as well as foreign languages, pottery, painting and music in great variety. Fresh Horizons students, as already noted, were well acquainted with this extended provision and had made good use of it.

In the best of these new-type evening institutes and in the day-time classes that were increasingly, although inadequately, provided, students could thus choose from a greatly extended range of single subjects and piece them together if they so wished in a pattern dictated only by personal preferences. The City Lit, with its less usual and more specialized range of literary and artistic offerings, catered also, in the main, for the single-subject student, although among the day-time clientele, as already indicated, there were people constructing full-day programmes for themselves from the separate elements of the prospectus.

Courses offered by the WEA and the university extra-mural departments were also based on single subjects in so far as they were non-vocational and non-certificate, as most of them were. Students might choose to take more than one subject at a time but the choice and the mixture, again, were their own. There was, moreover, a strongly urged democratic procedure for the building of individual WEA courses: tutors and students were expected to agree the syllabus together. Ideally this could only be done if the group was well established before the opening of the course but, in common practice, the proposed subject had first to be advertised, and it was largely on the basis of this publicity that a class was formed at the opening meeting of the course. In the meantime a book-list had been prepared by the tutor who, if a supply of books was to arrive before the class ended, had already seen to it that they were ordered. T. S. Eliot, as yet a relatively unknown poet, faced with a university extra-mural class that had come together to study nineteenth-century literature, managed to persuade its members that their real interest lay in the seventeenth, which was what he preferred to talk about.[1] He was certainly not unique: less distinguished tutors have made shifts in the programme, perhaps not quite so drastic, to suit their own interests and specialisms.

Within any chosen theme there can, of course, always be variations, and skilful tutors learn how to play them to the growing involvement of the students and their own scholarship. The most satisfying classes are probably those in which tutor and students move forward together on an expanding frontier of knowledge with sometimes tutor and sometimes students setting the pace and direction.

Flexible planning

In talking to prospective students about the Fresh Horizons courses, their package-deal character was always emphasized. Applicants who were reluctant to accept this were advised of other courses they might consider. But within the framework of the courses as a whole, syllabuses of the separate elements were guidelines rather than set programmes and this needed to be so. Each group had an individual character and groups progressed at different rates. Tutors varied their techniques, improvising and experimenting in trying to make their courses more effective. The planning of each element had to allow for adaptations and flexible handling, but planning there had to be: students were quick to detect when a tutor was resorting to unprepared expedients and living, as it were, from hand to mouth.

The requirement to take the course as a whole and the acceptance of the conditions by applicants did not mean that, in the outcome, every component found equal enthusiasm. Students were sometimes disappointed that a subject did not live up to their hopeful image of it; sometimes they were surprised to find a liking for a subject they had hitherto rejected. The idea of trying, in any degree, to impose an acceptance of the whole course on a student could not be tenable in view of the voluntary character of an undertaking to study, in adult life, and the loose bonds that exist between providers and takers in adult education. The extent to which students did accept the less immediately palatable parts of the course was a mark of their commitment. But they indicated their preferences and it is useful to look at these fairly closely.

The relative popularity of the different elements of the part-time courses, throughout the period, is shown in two ways: first, by an examination of the registers of attendances for each subject which reveal to what extent students voted with their feet, for or against a subject, and second, through replies given by students, who completed questionnaires, to a question about the values derived from separate aspects of the course.

The lower average attendance in some subjects as shown in Table 14 indicates a total drop-out from that part of the course by some students. Although attempts were made to unravel the difficulties that led to it, it was inevitable that this would occur from time to time. Often, however, the drop-out was not complete and intermittent attendance made it difficult for the tutor to carry through a planned programme, especially in speech and drama, and created breaks in continuity that irritated students who stayed with the course. It should be stressed, however, that evidence of lower popularity of any part of the course with some students conceals the genuine pleasure and satisfaction of others. Moreover, when students were unenthusiastic about a subject or some aspect of it, they would, nevertheless, often admit that it was good for them to have to face up to it.

Table 14 *All part-time day and evening students—average percentage attendances by subject*

| | percentage attendances | |
| | day students | evening students |
subjects	1966–73	1968–73
	%	%
English Literature	65·1	66·2
English—Spoken and Written	63·8	65·1
Social Studies	60·0	64·0
Speech and Drama	56·3	59·1
Mathematics	56·2	N.A.
Tutorial periods	61·6	N.A.

Students were asked in the questionnaire, 'Would you now say, in relation to the subjects studied on the course, of what value you have since found them, if any.' It is clear from the replies that many, probably a majority, answered in terms of a general assessment of the value they attached to having studied the subject, or even of the pleasure derived at the time, rather than the specific value derived since. This raises the question of the quantitative validity of the results, since students who answered the question literally may have valued or enjoyed the subject at the time but have been careful to answer in the light of its subsequent perceived utility, and, in fact, some made this distinction in their replies. The confusion raises, but gives no answer to, some interesting speculations about the relationship between enjoyment and perseverance in learning and its ultimate perceived value. For the present purpose the answers were accepted at their face value and were analysed under the three heads of 'much', 'some' and 'little or none'. 'No answer' was also recorded and summarized. People expressed themselves with varying degrees of emphasis and lower, rather than higher, ratings were given to the replies within the categories indicated and summarized in Table 15.

The general ranking agreement between the questionnaire responses and the attendance records does seem to indicate a considerable consensus of opinion among students. More detailed consideration of the separate subject areas, the ways they were handled and students' comments provide some clues as to the reasons for it, remembering, however, that the attendance records reveal differences of only 7 per cent between the best and the worst attended subjects among evening students and approximately 9 per cent among day students.

Table 15 *Respondents on part-time courses expressing opinions as to subsequent value of subjects studied (percentages)*

| | day students | | | | evening students | | | |
| | claiming value as: (N:112) | | | | claiming value as: (N:80) | | | |
subject area	much	some	little	N.A.	much	some	little	N.A.
	%	%	%	%	%	%	%	%
English Literature	25	61	4	10	25	58	10	8
English Spoken & Written	19	59	9	13	26	56	9	9
Social Studies	15	56	13	16	25	46	23	6
Speech and Drama	7	42	28	23	24	36	21	19
Mathematics	13	31	24	32	–	–	–	–

Literature and language

Of the subjects in the programme, it is clear that literature and language were the most popular. The evidence in the replies assessed numerically, is supported by students' added comments and by the record of attendances. English Language was described in the prospectus as 'English, spoken and written' and was handled with a fair degree of flexibility and experiment. It called for a policy rather than a structure but the policy needed to be supported by structural elements. Of those elements, grammar needed least attention. The tutor had sometimes to demonstrate that there was no justification for the amount of formal teaching (and confusion) that would ensue in trying to establish the vocabulary of grammar, by getting the students to accept how rare was real non-grammatical usage among them. Students' individual grammatical solecisms were dealt with during their own tutorials. If there was a fairly common difficulty throughout the group it was made the subject of comment and discussion in the class meeting. Grammar, spelling and punctuation were related as much as possible to their historical evolution to underline how much these were matters of usage and convention, without decrying the need for respecting accepted standards.

The customary formal elements of the use of English as an examination subject—précis, comprehension and essay writing—were handled as tools to be used in the course and in subsequent studies. Learning how to summarize a chapter was more important than making a two hundred word précis; comprehension was getting to know how to read for different purposes and in different ways, closely sometimes to extract underlying implications, and at other times scanning to isolate information. Writing of all kinds, descriptive, analytical and imaginative, in class and out of it, was urged and its importance constantly stressed. Short pieces were set to begin with but the aim was that before the end of the course a student would be able to produce an extended essay of five thousand words or a chapter of autobiography of similar length.

Essays were set in social studies and in literature and each tutor was responsible for marking these in relation to structure, use of language, sentence construction and spelling as well as content. All were teachers of English; if a student needed extra help, special written work was set.

In a similar way all were concerned in the teaching of study techniques, though this was particularly emphasized in the English language course. The City Lit librarian helped with talks on retrieval of information, the use of a library and its resources. Oracy, too, was implicit in every part of the course through discussion and individual spoken contributions. In the English class there were brains trusts, impromptu speeches and small group discussion with student rapporteurs.

After the first term's immersion in techniques in the English class it was often found useful to tie in, perhaps in alternate weeks, a series of talks on the history of the English language. This served to knit together some of the fragments of English history that lingered with the students from their schooldays, or derived from their own reading or viewing of television drama, and set them in a new and, it was hoped, coherent framework. The changing character of the language from Old English through to modern times provided reading material in class and anticipated the difficulties students might have in subsequent studies, in reading prose and poetry of earlier centuries.

This linked up with the literature course in which the tutors aimed at securing for the students as wide an experience as possible of the range of English literature, realizing, at the same time, that they would need help in tackling idioms of previous eras. The completed study of a Shakespearean tragedy was not only satisfying as an aesthetic and emotional experience but was a significant intellectual achievement for those who had never done it before. Those who had met Shakespeare at school now recognized in themselves a higher level of understanding arising out of their own maturity. Several times the reading of a play was done intensively on a residential weekend course when the problems of language and the meaning of the text could be teased out in small groups and a reading performance achieved by the whole party, by the end of Sunday afternoon. Students were also grouped for, say, the reading at home of a Victorian novel, with a requirement to examine a particular aspect of the work and follow it through. Members of each group pooled their observations in class and so made available to each other and to the whole of the class the experience gained from the reading. In this way the significance of different elements of the work came to light that were helpful in securing closer reading and study of the text and mobilizing material for essays. Poems and short stories came in for similar treatment, the poems being read in class and the short stories at home. They were useful entry points for the course, ensuring that students were plunged into a reading and discussion programme from the start. Tutors were rarely lecturers; their task was to plan the course and devise the methods and then, as much as possible, to draw the groups into a discovery of the value of the works being studied, urging new points on them, filling in the gaps and providing a background of reference to the whole study.

Comments in the questionnaires rarely showed indifference to this part of the course and, very frequently, enthusiasm for it.

'I always liked reading and it was very stimulating to work as a group on the different books.'
'Experience in essay-writing and close rather than superficial study.'
'An enjoyment of Shakespeare's works.'
'Enabled me to tackle "A" level and Extra-Mural Diploma course.'
'Opened up completely new experience.'
'Great upsurge of reading in depth.'
'A whole new life.'

Social studies

Consideration of the social and historical situation in which a work of literature appeared frequently tied in with aspects of the social studies course, the conduct of which was a much harder tutorial assignment. The sociologist's task of categorizing and quantifying aspects of society is alienating to many adults who can sympathize with the emotional and intellectual problems of a Hamlet or a Maggie Tulliver but resent the rationalization of elements contained in their problems. It was also asking for trouble to become embroiled in social classifications at an early stage in the course unless the tutor was very experienced in handling the personal reactions that this produced. One tutor said she only felt the group come to life when she mentioned the social aspects of divorce in the third meeting and found she had a class of experts. But the difficulty then arose of leading the discussion on to general issues without letting individual personal experiences absorb the time available.

The attendance summary shows social studies as occupying fourth place (out of five) in the eight years of day-time classes and the third (out of four) in the six years of evening ones. It is difficult to dissociate this connection from the varying personalities and experience of adult teaching, sometimes non-existent, of the nine tutors who were engaged at different times throughout the period. A year-by-year breakdown shows that only in one year did the attendances reach first and second place. The comments of

Valerie Hall, the first full-time and most successful tutor in this subject, are worth recording:

'There are two problems confronting the social studies tutor on Fresh Horizons courses—a potential hostility in the students' perception of the meaning and purpose of social studies and the difficulties inherent in establishing a balance between objectivity and subjectivity in a discipline which is increasingly questioning its own scientific basis. The hostility is generated in part by a confusion in students' minds of sociology with socialism (and its more radical implications) and also as a result of the natural defensiveness of a group of people who are suddenly asked to question, albeit systematically, the very basic assumptions which give meaning to their lives. On the one hand the tutor wants to begin where the students are at in their own lives; on the other, his purpose is to familiarize the students with perspectives which may cast their experience in a different light. In some way he must overcome any manifest or latent hostility and construct a framework of enquiry which allows the student to stand back from his or her own position in society, while at the same time not invalidating the ways in which the individual makes sense of that position.

'In order to overcome these challenges, the method of teaching takes supremacy over the content. It is tempting for the social science graduate to teach what he was taught and he is encouraged in this temptation by the ready acquiescence of adult students in a style of teaching that reassures them they are getting a body of knowledge hitherto inaccessible. Too often, further pressure is applied by the knowledge that, if the student wants to go on to higher education, demonstration of the acquisition of a particular type of knowledge may be judged as more important than the development of positive critical faculties.

'The solution can be found in the tutor's ability and willingness to capitalize on the temporary removal of the individual student from the usual routines of his or her home and work environments. The insecurity and vulnerability which results from the initial disruption of their taken-for-granted everyday lifestyles can be turned to positive advantage in encouraging the student to reflect on the ways in which that lifestyle has been shaped, its relationship to other lifestyles and the social structure as a whole.

'For the social studies tutor who has faith in the ultimate goal of encouraging questions, rather than providing answers, who is concerned as much with the student's self-discovery as the discoveries of others, there is a ready-made course structure in the individual's personal history and the processes which have shaped its development. The natural sequence of an individual's life from childhood through school and adolescence to work and parenthood can be considered within a framework of social-scientific enquiry which encourages the student to be an anthropologist in his own society. The ways in which social scientists have tried to describe and explain how society works become the pegs upon which to hang the student's own exploration of the meanings he has traditionally assigned to both his own and others' actions.

'The scepticism which is fundamental to the social scientific understanding of human behaviour can be harnessed to the student's own propensity to self-doubt, so that both are transformed into a powerful weapon for questioning, on the one hand established opinion in the social sciences (and thereby acquiring knowledge of that opinion) and, on the other, the origins and nature of the meanings they bring to their own self-evaluations. In that way, social studies become a crucial tool in discovering the "fresh" horizons they are seeking.'

Social studies need not and should not be approached only through sociology. Within the living experience of a group of students ranging in age from the mid-20s to late 50s or more, an historical viewpoint can be reached, and the causes and significance of economic change explored. Some tutors encouraged the writing and reading of personal and family histories that illustrated these elements, particularly those spanning several generations and extending into the other national cultures that were frequently represented in the classes.

In making their own assessments of value derived from social studies, students commented on the widening of their range of interests and the enlightenment they received on social problems, e.g.

'That subject was an absolute eye-opener. It made me more critical of politics and society.'
'It made me aware of problems I didn't know existed.'

The course had its influence on subsequent choices and was seen as useful on social work and other courses, e.g.

'I chose sociology as an option at college.'
'Very useful—have re-used material on my social work course.'
'Good grounding for the Open University.'
It also had immediate practical applications, e.g.
'It removed sentimentality—I'm now more practical as a voluntary worker.'
'I became a tutor for the Cambridge House literacy scheme.'

Speech and Drama

Speech and drama, in later courses designated voice, speech and movement, also proved relatively less popular than other subjects. The tutors had a difficult task, not made any easier by the fact that the students they usually taught opted for the subject from either a very acute knowledge of need or an already developed interest in self-expression. Where most of the Fresh Horizons students would willingly have chosen a literature course as a normal adult education option, many of them would not have faced a voluntary plunge into the deskless open space that the drama class required. It took an effort for them to see this as contributing to their development, or, to accept it, knowing that it might. Some tutors were more successful than others in overcoming the diffidence of students without pressuring them, but a dissident group or a non-cooperating person in the class created problems that sapped the will of the class as a whole. It raises the question whether a more subtle involvement in oral and physical effort would not have been a better solution than a specifically designated subject. In subsequent courses other approaches have, in fact, been tried. However, although judging from the questionnaire replies, this subject was the least appreciated, half the respondents recorded some benefit from it, e.g.

'Helped bring me out.'
'Helped to overcome shyness.'
'Helped me to feel more confident.' (A comment made many times.)
'Breathing and relaxation exercises were helpful.'
'Relaxed my inhibitions for movement lessons at college.'
'Greater appreciation of theatre and radio.'

but

'I was too inhibited to enjoy this.'

Mathematics

The mathematics course produced its problems too. After the first year the class was taken by the same tutor throughout. He had to combat, which he did with infinite patience, the mental blockages that all but a few students brought with them. It seemed that those who had survived even fairly simple levels of numeracy without trauma, at an earlier stage of life, strode through the new approach with confidence. Indeed, they sometimes found the repetitions and explanations demanded by the others tedious.

The subject was also one in which a break in attendance could mean the missing of a few necessary steps in understanding. For the student of literature, a partial comprehension may be frustrating but there is still value and pleasure to be derived from what is understood. For the student of mathematics, at least at an early stage, a partial understanding only frustrates. It might have solved some difficulties if there had been the resources to divide students into two groups, making fast and slow streams for this subject, after, say, the first half-term.

A perceptive student from the 1967–8 day course put her finger on some of the problems that persisted throughout:

'In chapter 2 of the New Maths book one was introduced to number systems without numbers and to the algebra of logic. This however meant nothing to me until one day in the social studies class, we were shown how it was possible to talk in the abstract about groups and partial overlap, etc. It would help immensely if the inter-related phases of maths and social studies followed one another, i.e. one week only between the relevant phases in each subject. The phase in the social studies class on language came just about the right time. This coincided with what we were doing at the time on the history of the English language.'

Yet many students did find new satisfactions in grappling with the subject even if this was sometimes more related to knowing what the mystery was about than to the attainment of a mastery. Appreciative comments included:

'Grasped maths for the first time.'
'See everything now in a different light and help my children with their new maths.'
'None—except I know now what my god-children are talking about.'
'Not a foreign language any more.'
'Immense value—has awakened an interest in a subject I thought I could never attempt.'
'Helped a lot when I went to a college of education.'
'Appreciated it in my local government finance work.'
(student who was a borough alderman)
'Useful for the HND course I am now studying.'

An extract from a letter sent by a student who 'had always been poor in this subject' describing an interview for a place on a university social administration course makes a wryly amusing pendant:

'I was told "you're OK in general for the course but economics comes into it: can you read a graph?" I answered "Do you mean histograms and frequency polygons?" He said "If you know those I won't go any further. You can do the course". I didn't add that I didn't know about them till I did the Fresh Horizons course but that's the truth.'

There was not time within the six hours a week of the evening course to include an obligatory mathematics element, but a twelve-week course of one-and-a-half hours a week on similar lines was added to the general Whit and Mid-summer terms' programmes of the City Lit, largely for the benefit of the students who had taken the evening Fresh Horizons course. But coming as this did after the main course had ended and within the holiday season, the take-up was only moderate. The course had to be encompassed in half the time allowed in the day-time Fresh Horizons package and the pace proved too fast for many of the students who attempted it. For others it was a glimpse of a possible future enlightenment. They report that their interest was stimulated, but their concentration could not be sustained. Nevertheless, one student commented, 'I took this before the main course and it greatly increased my confidence.'

Undoubtedly the Mathematics course made its case better as an integral part of the main Fresh Horizons package than as an addendum to it. Though many day students regretted that their blockages refused to go away, others were pleasantly relieved that they responded to new treatment and, within the whole programme, a feeling of frustration in one part of it could be compensated for by the success felt in another.

Consideration had to be given in promoting the courses to the loss of those recruits for whom mathematics was the ultimate deterrent. As there were seldom places to spare on the courses, recruitment did not suffer and applicants could be given help in making other choices. But in considering people for admission to the course, the mathematics obligation did act as a test of serious intent and there was evidence that in tackling unfamiliar and what appeared to be uncongenial, aspects of learning, students did secure unexpected insights and satisfactions.

Linkages

In meeting students' problems it was useful to bear in mind some words of I. A. Richards:[2]

> The prime obstacle in general education is a feeling of helplessness before the unintelligible. Every problem is new to the mind which first meets it and it is baffling until he can recognize something in it which he has met and dealt with already. . . . The teacher meets with all this whenever he reads anything that stretches his intelligence: the pupil meets with it all the time and, if he is being well-taught, he should be expecting it and enjoying the sense of increasing power that his progressive mastery of it can afford. . . . This growth in power is fundamentally the vitalising incentive with which education builds.

He goes on to say, 'The unintelligibility of a problem . . . most often is due to the language in which the problem comes to us' and this is, undoubtedly, part of the difficulty that an adult student, in particular, has in coming to terms with the principles of mathematics.

It might have been useful to have made a linked approach, associating mathematics with social studies, rather than basing it on a theoretical understanding. But the whole question of team work had to be seen in relation to the tutorial set-up of the courses. Throughout the period, apart from the final year when a full-time course was established and one other short exception, all the tutors, including the tutor-organizer, were engaged part-time only. 'Part-time' in this context means an engagement for the actual hours of class contact over a period of two or three terms according to the length of the course. The tutor might have had other classes within the City Lit, for which a separate contract would be in force, or might be attending solely for the one-and-a-half hours a week that he or she was teaching on a Fresh Horizons course.

Cost and time of travel and time spent in preparation and marking, were regarded as being paid for within the hourly rate that applied for the actual time spent in the class-room. Tutors were subject specialists who had become involved in this essentially team commitment. The closed subject approach was, therefore, almost inevitable and cross-fertilization between different elements in the programme and co-operation between tutors in relation to syllabuses, students' difficulties and progress was not easy to achieve. The tutor-organizer was the link-woman but she had no direct allocation of time for this and had to devise means of securing liaison as best she could.

For the first two day-time courses duplicate notebooks were used in which each tutor kept a record of class-work and tasks set week by week. The carbon copy of each tutor's record was passed to the tutor-organizer weekly for circulation to the other tutors. As additional courses were added and student numbers increased, such an exchange of information became difficult to keep alive. Tutors often had to rush away after a class and it might be another week before they appeared again. Some tutors voluntarily reported on students' work and progress; others had to be sought out, sometimes with difficulty. At the beginning of each course, the tutor-organizer circulated to all tutors a summary of information about students derived from their application forms and initial interviews and supplemented this with further notes from time to time. By such means and by chance encounters in the staff-room and coffee-bar, some sort of contact was kept. Eventually approval was given for tutors to be paid for up to three meetings a year to discuss the courses and students' progress on them. Though it was not easy to get all the tutors together at one time—and even a meeting-place could be difficult to find in the overcrowded building—this, with continuing informal contacts, proved an essential element in maintaining the design and purpose of the courses.

Problems of team-teaching are not entirely solved by the appointment of full-time staff. Payment difficulties do not arise, but contact may be difficult if the tutors have a heavy teaching load spread over morning, afternoon and evening sessions. Subject competence may be limited within the staff and so enforce a curriculum based on available resources rather than on what is judged wholly desirable; part-time staff recruited to enlarge resources may not be easily integrated within the team.

The reluctance of some tutors to move out from the safe framework of formal teaching (or, what is even more inhibiting, lecturing) and welcome the less obvious but more demanding role of facilitator of students' learning in an adult education setting, is something that has to be fought and overcome. Students appreciate the competence of their tutors within their subject specialisms and may be dazzled by a brilliant display of expertise whether in the mode of presentation or in the choice of the material presented. But their chief satisfaction and probably the only one they finally recognize, is that which comes from the steps they take by themselves, hand-in-hand with a tutor whose pace is geared to theirs.

In short, it cannot be too strongly emphasized that, in a course where the concern is for people rather than subjects, except in so far as subjects are essentially related to the needs of students, it is quite vital to have time and staffing standards to allow for adequate consultation among tutors. It is all the more a tribute to the part-time tutors who worked on these and subsequent Fresh Horizons courses and the interest aroused in them by their special nature that they voluntarily contributed the extra effort that succeeded in creating such a satisfying outcome for so many of their students.

Making it known

It is one thing to devise a course: another thing to attract students to it.

The Inner London Education Authority produces *Floodlight*, a classified guide of 150 pages to all its part-time day and evening classes, which is on sale at bookstalls from the late summer onwards each year. It is well known and widely used. The City Lit's own publicity centres mainly round the wide distribution of its autumn and summer prospectuses and the missionary zeal of satisfied clients.

These were in the beginning, and continued to be, important sources of information to the general public about the courses. But the trouble with the grape vine is that it produces fruit to type. Over the years approaches by other methods reached newer groups of potential students and their cumulative influence contributed to the firm establishment of the courses.

The questionnaire asked, 'How did you hear about the course?' An analysis of the replies is given in Table 16.

Table 16 *How respondents heard about part-time courses* (*percentages*)

	women			men		all	
information source	day 1966–9	day 1970–3	evening 1968–73	day 1966–73	evening 1968–73	day	evening
N =	49	56	53	(7)	27	112	80
	%	%	%		%	%	%
City Lit prospectus	26	16	36	(3)	29	22	34
Floodlight	2	–	13	(1)	19	2	15
friend/relative	14	21	27	(1)	29	18	28
counselling	–	7	6	–	8	3	6
press	35	28	7	(1)	15	30	10
radio/TV	8	16	4	–	–	12	2
other (inc. library)	14	12	7	(1)	–	13	5

Though there were no separate funds available for publicity, the tutor-organizer promoted general press releases with the help of the education authority's press department and made personal contact with journalists and broadcasters who showed an interest in the venture.

An indication is given in Chapter 9 how newspaper and magazine articles aiming, from the point of view of journalistic practice, at a timely impact at the start of the autumn term could rebound on the organizers of the courses and create disappointment to enquirers who found the class already full or recruits who made too hasty a decision to join.

Only in one year, so far as could be discovered, did a general press release hit the pages of a popular daily. At least one dissatisfied young man started a new career in teaching as a direct result. The quality papers can be fairly sure that their readers are likely to be interested in education. A succinct note in the *Guardian* in the summer of 1972 created a demand that almost filled a whole day-time class. A profile of that paper's readership might have predicted that this group would attain the highest completion rate of any under review—91 per cent, with over two-thirds of the students making 80 per cent of all possible attendances.

BBC 'Woman's Hour' and 'You and Yours' also spread the news widely on odd occasions. With the coming of local radio, broadcast publicity could be focused within the catchment area of the City Lit. BBC's Radio London, which has an established connection with the Inner London Education Authority's community education service, proved an invaluable ally during the later courses. The voices of satisfied students heard in interviews and discussions over the air gave a reassuring stimulus to otherwise uncertain enquirers.

But such methods reached day-time students best. Fresh Horizons evening students, less in the habit of reading newspapers and with less time for radio listening, recorded a much slighter influence from the media. Their sources of information were much more the City Lit prospectus, the influence of friends and *Floodlight*.

But news spreads in less conventional ways. One respondent records hearing about the course 'at a jumble sale' and another 'from a passenger in my taxi'.

7
The counselling element

Fresh Horizons students displayed the variety that can be found in any adult group seeking educational satisfaction and drawn randomly from a large population. In attempting to meet their needs, this diversity of age, early education, occupation and life experience had to be reckoned with. But over and above the normal expectations of adult students they were being offered a chance to rethink and, perhaps, reshape their lives. Even if some members of the group remained firmly concerned only with the immediate learning experience, they were affected by the restless searching that went on around them. The nature of the course led them to become conscious of their past educational experiences as well as of their present and future needs. Many were already acutely aware of an early educational loss; others, with their formal education brought into the forefront of their minds, began to re-examine and reassess the circumstances surrounding it. Some indication has already been given of how they felt their schooling had been interrupted, curtailed or prematurely laid aside not only by war and post-war disruption but also by either their own or their parents' actions.

Out of the 192 part-time students who replied to the questionnaire, over two-thirds felt they had been handicapped educationally by social, family or personal circumstances. Table 17 shows the extent to which they felt different factors were responsible for this.

The analysis demonstrates the way in which national events or social policies of a receding past project their influences through

Table 17 *Respondents—reported sources of educational handicaps*

		women (Pt-T)			men (Pt-T)		
		day		evening		day	eveining
sources of handicap	N =	N 105	%	N 53	%	N 7	N 27 (%)
war/evacuation		26	(25)	7	(13)	1	8 (29)
11+/streaming		7	(7)	6	(11)	1	3 (11)
family							
parents' separation		4	(4)	2	(4)	2	3 (11)
parents' illness/death		6	(6)	2	(4)	–	4 (15)
removals		14	(13)	6	(11)	1	1 (4)
poverty		6	(6)	3	(5)	–	2 (7)
sub-total		30	(29)	13	(24)	3	10 (37)
personal							
illness		10	(9)	7	(13)	1	2 (7)
left-hand		5	(5)	2	(4)	1	1 (4)
physical		2	(2)	–		–	–
stammer		1	(1)	–		–	1 (4)
sub-total		18	(17)	9	(17)	2	4 (15)
various		11	(10)	5	(9)	2	2 (7)
total handicaps reported		92		40		9	27
numbers affected		72	(69)	33	(62)	6	20 (74)

the lifetimes of those who experienced them. In times of rapid change, such as the present, they will continue to do so in different forms and different ways. But additionally, there will always be family and personal reasons why childhood disadvantage continues to hamper adult development and leads to frustration and the need for remedial action. The Fresh Horizons students noted family break-up (an increasing element in the lives of today's children), childhood illness, parental ignorance and inhibiting personal defects as reasons why their early education stopped short of what they later recognized as their potential. The following quotations from questionnaire replies supplement those concerned with war-time educational hazards in Chapter 3. They are not drawn from totally disadvantaged people coming from a wholly crippling environment but from a normal intake of adult men and women meeting day-to-day responsibilities with often more than general competence. The experience described should therefore be considered all the more significant in relation to our concern for the population at large.

Eleven-plus rejection and streaming

'After failing the 11-plus I felt labelled and very inferior.'
>(Woman aged 36: left secondary modern school at 15)

'11-plus failure led to lack of confidence: I felt doomed to failure.'
>(Woman aged 30: left private school at 15)

'After failing 11-plus I was put in the "E" form of a secondary modern school. This upset me a great deal as my brother and sister went to grammar schools. I rose to the "B" form by the third year but I put little effort into the work and because I couldn't get a job, stayed on to do two "O"s but didn't pass.'
>(Man aged 23 who, incidentally, obtained two 'A's and four 'O's by correspondence study after leaving school and before starting Fresh Horizons evening course, concurrently with which and while working full-time, he studied for 'A' level sociology, which he passed with A grade. After the course took a degree course in sociology)

'As far as I can recall I was a border-line failure for the 11-plus. I went to a secondary modern school and did fairly well, coming top three times in a row between the second and third years but the teachers involved and the headmaster felt I would not be able to cope in a higher class. I was very disappointed because I had worked hard as the higher classes were studying for GCE. By the fourth year I had dropped back even in the subjects I had enjoyed.'
>(Woman aged 25: left secondary modern school at 15)

Changing schools

'My parents moved: I took the same scholarship exam twice, passed to a central school and, after one term on each occasion, I had to leave. Eventually I finished up at an elementary school as my parents didn't get a transfer to a comparable school and I left at the age of 14.'
>(Woman aged 56)

'Constant change from one school to another meant missing a number of actual terms: some subjects were never even started.'

(Woman aged 44)

Economic necessity

'Taken away from boarding school at sixteen due to lack of funds—no exam certificate and saw no chance of further education.'

(Woman aged 48)

Parents' death

'My father died and I had to leave school at 14.'

(Man aged 48)

'I was preparing for matric when my mother died, so returned to my aunt in Wales who suggested nursing. The three cousins I grew up with all went to university while I struggled on as a nursery nurse.'

(Woman aged 42)

'Death of father. Disturbed mother needing constant attention and therefore bad adolescence. Pressure on one to earn money and strict feelings against self-education from parent.'

(Woman aged 35)

Childhood illness

'I had TB in the lung when I was eight and spent four years in hospitals and convalescent homes. I missed nearly five years of schooling. I missed so much that I had no foundation on which to build when I returned to school—a very bad secondary one. The first year was terrible as I didn't understand anything. When I left a few days after my fifteenth birthday I was top in English and French, but even though I've done "O" levels since and an "A" level (by correspondence), I still feel a great gap in my education. I sometimes feel I will never overcome the handicap of the loss of those years.'

(Woman aged 30)

Sex discrimination

'Choice between my brother and myself attending High
School (in Germany). I had to leave after one year so that he
could continue.'

(Woman aged 33)

'My father did not believe in educating girls beyond the age
required by law. My two brothers went on to university and
I resented this for many years.'

(Woman aged 44)

A wrong choice

'Parents not sufficiently interested to prevent a totally
disastrous series of educational and career choices after "O"
level. It is only now, ten to twelve years later that I am
correcting this by going to university which I should have
done years ago.'

(Man aged 27)

A change in the rules

'I was ready to take School Certificate at fourteen but
suddenly a change in the rules was brought in (the GCE
examinations which at first had a minimum age limit) and
you couldn't sit it till sixteen. So I left school rather than
submit to the boredom of two repetitive years.'

(Woman aged 37)

. . . and stlll the Schools Council tries to find the perfect school-
leaving certificate with apparently little thought for all those who
have gone before, or are part of the changeover.

Need for counselling

The students quoted were not unique in being only partially conscious of the extent of the educational revolution of the post-1944
years. Nor did they always appreciate how thinly spread the
opportunities had been earlier and that they were now in a limbo
for which they could not blame themselves. Yet blame themselves
they often did for not making better use of such opportunities as

they had had or for their indifference and lack of interest at school. The reproach of the school report 'could do better if she tried' still lingered on the consciences of many.

It seemed axiomatic, therefore, that by reason of their variety of backgrounds, needs and previous educational loss, the students would want information, advice and help tailored to their individual needs, and all the more so since they were exploring the possibilities of new careers or of entering higher education or training at a time of life beyond that normally assumed to be appropriate. The system as it exists is built round schools, colleges and the apparatus by which adolescents make their progress towards economic and social independence. Some very elementary knowledge can elude the adult trying to get back into it unaided: two examples illustrate the pitfalls.

The first concerns 'levels'; it is a very frequent source of surprise that one does not need 'O' level in a GCE subject before proceeding to 'A' level. The regulations do not say you have to but then again they do not say you need not. The regulations are written for schools; the schools know that it is not necessary but schools put their pupils through the examination procedures that belong to their age and stage; adults have to adapt a school system to their own needs. One wonders how many adults have enrolled themselves, year after year, in evening classes for a long haul of 'O's before embarking on the 'A's that might have served them better and been better suited to their maturity if, indeed, they were necessary at all. How many of those enrolling them see that they have the information—or even know they might need it?

A second example: a young man turned up at the City Lit, on the advice of the admissions tutor at a local polytechnic, to apply for enrolment in the Fresh Horizons course. It turned out that he had a bunch of 'O' levels and three 'A's all painfully achieved through correspondence or private study after a full day's work as a lorry driver. He had been turned down for entry to a degree course, after a cursory examination of his application, because his grades were not good enough—but at least he was given some advice as to where he might find some help. Among his 'O' levels was one in Latin, self-taught from scratch. When asked why he had bothered to take Latin he replied that it was a requirement of the degree course for which he had prepared and this was indeed so when he started his lone pilgrimage. In the meantime, the regulations, originally consulted in a public library, had been changed, but how does the self-propelled student come by such knowledge? By a fortunate chance he came within the range of advice and influence that was at least able to save him another wasted year, but how many more, like him, do waste important years following mistaken paths?

Counselling arrangements

From the start, therefore, the counselling needs of students were recognized, and efforts to satisfy them were built into the Fresh Horizons courses. The tutorial hour for the day-time students and the time set aside before class for the evening ones were evidence of this. When the full-time course was instituted in 1973, four hours were allocated in the weekly programme for group and individual tutorials and counselling for its twenty-five members. Students soon came to accept that this was as much an essential part of the course as the class periods in literature or mathematics. It was not merely that the tutors were there to be approached tentatively from time to time: it was a recognized part of the rela-tion between tutors and students. Although the set hours formal-ized this, it was inevitable and indeed desirable that counselling always overflowed the time nominally allowed for it, into lunch breaks, after class, on the stairs and in the corridors. Though the tutors appreciated the implied confidence, the need to be available not only absorbed much time but was also both intellectually and emotionally demanding.

Time was not only a problem for the tutors. Students had to cram counselling interviews, requests for tutorial help and the exploration of further opportunities into the already full day or evening programme. The lunch hour was purposely short for the day-time students to allow for an early return home. For the even-ing students, most of whom did not finish work before 5.30, classes began at 6 p.m., and ended at 9.15, with a coffee-break of a quarter of an hour only. Discussing this problem in relation to the New Opportunities courses at the University of Newcastle-upon-Tyne, the organizers write:

> The full day was made deliberately busy with only forty-five minutes for refreshments in a five and a quarter hour day.

> This involvement in group work is attractive but allows little time (even with generous staffing) for individual tutorials and counselling. We have to make time for this in the 'Opportunities' sessions but we are always aware that this is at the expense of other activities.[1]

But counselling time is expensive for the administration and can be so for the students. Competing for scarce resources within a tight budgeting scheme or established on a self-financing basis by charging fees to students, individual attention may become too costly to be acceptable. In an account of the counselling arrangements at the Women's Resource Centre of the University of British Columbia, the authors say:

> A major difficulty for women is lack of money they can call their own and it soon became clear that many women were not in a position to take advantage of opportunities for learning and growth because they did not feel they had the right to spend family income on themselves. This necessitated a change from traditional one-to-one counselling methods, and the development of a new plan, whereby educational counselling could be made available by means of programs and services.[2]

Using the more sophisticated language of the North American system this approach included 'group counselling by means of self-development courses', ' "peer" counselling by unpaid associates' and do-it-yourself techniques practised by students within the resources unit of the Centre.

The day courses

Group counselling became an inevitable and essential part of the Fresh Horizons courses which certainly could not boast of 'generous staffing'. The tutorial hour allowed time for this in the part-time day course but because of the varied uses to which the period was put, careful management was needed. There was no set pattern: it was an opportunity for the tutor to pull together the various elements within the whole course, and it provided a weekly check-point on the volume and intensity of effort being demanded by the tutorial staff, particularly with regard to the programme of essays, set-reading and other work in progress. It also provided a chance to sort out misunderstandings with the class as a whole and to find where satisfactions and dissatisfactions were arising. This hour had to be used also to look at further education and career prospects. Basic information was assembled for reference, but its use had always to take into account that it had rarely been compiled with adult needs in mind. Special arrangements for adults, where they existed, and the availability of local outlets had to be sought out. Students took part in this either individually or in groups, by assembling information on specific areas of career and training interest. Visiting specialists were invited to talk about careers prospects: in all these ways, tutors and students pooled their knowledge and experience. A resource centre for reference only would not have sufficed: students needed the opportunity for inter-action within the whole group and testified freely to its value.

But individual counselling was equally imperative whatever the difficulties. The tutorial hour, therefore, was also the time set for individual help and advice and because of the very full days, inter-views had to be arranged during class meetings. Sometimes the group would be working on a joint project while these consultations took place, or a programme of group discussions was set up on themes chosen by the group, the discussion being led by members in turn—it was always necessary to arrange for at least one under-study to the leader for the day, to allow for unavoidable absences and sudden Freudian illnesses. During this time the tutor could withdraw students for personal interviews. The aim was to see each student at least once a term, but any student could ask for a personal talk at any time in the course and this facility was regularly invoked.

Within the individual counselling sessions students could and did bring up personal and family difficulties, but they were advised where to seek appropriate help if they raised problems needing specialist advice outside the terms of the course. Knowing that the problem existed helped tutors to see students' needs as a whole and a quarter of the students completing questionnaires agreed that counselling on the course had been helpful in resolving personal difficulties.

The evening courses

There was no class tutorial hour set aside for the evening students but opportunity was taken, from time to time, in the tutor-organizer's class meeting, to review the opportunities open to students, to discuss post-course 'market prospects' and to take soundings on the progress of the course itself. Again, the filtering of information through the experience of students was part of the continuous build-up of an information and advice service. The evening students were more ready than the day-time ones to make an immediate jump into new career training or into higher education. They were more footloose and ready to take off when the course was over but there were still agonizing reappraisals. Some students were hesitant to commit themselves to a course of action that would put a strain on a deeply felt relationship; for others it meant giving up a job that had immediate financial satisfactions or prospects for life on a grant and an uncertain come-back in the end. Sometimes the question was whether to marry or not: one student records, 'probably deferred marriage indefinitely' as a decision made while on the course, and others left as their marriage plans crystallized.

To make sure that evening students had a chance of individual consultations with the tutor-organizer, a list was circulated in class early in the first term with dates and times of the set evening counselling hours, 4.45–6.45 on two evenings a week, and students were asked to sign themselves in for half-hour appointments. This was repeated in the second term but, again, this was far from being the whole involvement; many other encounters took place during and after classes and after—sometimes long after—a course had finished.

Students' evaluation of counselling

Although counselling was conceived as integral, it was not presented as the central element in the courses. To find out to what extent it had, in fact, turned out to be an important part of the course for the students and how it had affected their decision-making, they were asked to say, in completing the questionnaire, whether they agreed or disagreed with a number of statements about it. Table 18 shows that the most heavily endorsed was 'It was an essential part of the course' with agreement exceeding disagreement in a ratio of more than twenty to one. Only nine people affirmed that they were not really aware of it and only eleven that it had led to expectations that had created disappointment—a danger that always lurked in the background. Approximately half the respondents, the men rather more emphatically than the women, affirmed that counselling had helped them to be more aware of possibilities and their applicability to themselves. The statement, 'It helped me to sort out personal problems rationally', elicited less affirmative responses but still secured agreement from nearly one quarter of the respondents, indicating that, although solving personal difficulties was not the primary intention of the counselling service offered, it did, in fact, contribute to doing so.

Table 18 *Endorsements by all respondents—agree/disagree with statements regarding counselling on the course*

statement	women (Pt-T)				men (Pt-T)			
	agree		disagree		agree		disagree	
	no.	(%)	no.	(%)	no.	(%)	no.	(%)
It made me aware of possibilities I did not know of	79	(50)	13	(8)	24	(73)	–	(–)
It made me aware of possibilities I did not at first think applied to me	77	(49)	16	(10)	20	(59)	1	(3)
It led me to find out more about possibilities for myself	70	(44)	15	(9)	21	(62)	2	(6)
It helped me to sort out my expectations rationally	73	(46)	10	(6)	19	(56)	3	(9)
It helped me to sort out personal problems rationally	36	(23)	33	(21)	10	(29)	7	(21)
It was an essential part of the course	105	(66)	5	(3)	27	(79)	–	(–)
I was not really aware of it	7	(4)	75	(47)	2	(6)	20	(59)
It led to expectations which created disappointment	8	(5)	60	(38)	3	(9)	15	(44)

NB Differences between day and evening course students and those recruited in different years are too small to be worth distinguishing them

Mutual counselling

It was obvious from the discussions that went on in class and in the canteen and coffee-bar that students helped each other to find solutions to their problems. Replies to a question on this showed four-fifths of the evening students and nearly one-third of the part-time day students aware of such mutual support. On the face of it, the difference is curious since the day students had a longer time together and shared a lunch break. It is perhaps related to the greater certainty with which, on the whole, the evening students could consider making changes in their lives and would be immediately ready with information for each other about applications, interviews and strategies. Another clue lies in one reply as to how this happened—'In the pub. At the parties and at Fresh Horizons weekends'. Clubability varied considerably from course to course. Some Christmas and end-of-course parties approached riot proportions whereas others merely provided opportunity for a cooler friendly dispersal and farewell. Because of the need to hurry home to their families, day students were less free to join in social activities with each other than evening ones.

Some questionnaire replies (the first four from day and the last two from evening students), indicate typical ways in which students felt they had helped one another:

'It helped me a great deal to find there were other women with the same sort of problems as I had. I think we all gained a lot of confidence through the tutorials and discussing the possibilities that we were confronted with. However, personal discussions were not carried on with the whole class—people formed their own friendship groups. I was close to about five or six people and it was with them that such discussions took place.'

'By discussing our difficulties together I found I was not the only confused person in the world but was in fact quite normal. I don't think I solved any problems but I felt much better.'

'Hearing someone else talk about what they intended to do, made one feel "Yes, perhaps" and "I could do that too" or "Rather you than I".'

'Others were learning how to study. Everyone had difficulties and we encouraged and advised each other.'

'I was given reading matter by other students to help me. Informal talks gave me a deeper insight into methods and approaches concerning application. I gained much encouragement (and gave it too) and inspiration.'

'I found one student who, like me, was doing the course for entirely selfish reasons. That made me feel a little less frivolous. I became aware of other ways of life, expectations, chips on shoulders and it was good to get away from my own circle of acquaintances—pleasant though that is.'

Problems of the system

The really difficult problems came from outside the learning and counselling situation of the courses and crucially from the difficulties of fitting students into the regular system of entry to higher education, training and employment. It was clear that mature students were a curious anomaly as far as most institutions of higher education were concerned, though the colleges of education had by that time got round to making special arrangements for them. Elsewhere, even when it was written into the constitution and provision had been made for special entry tests unlinked to GCE performance, admissions tutors could be automatically dismissive on receipt of an application or brusquely unbelieving at interview.

The demand for evidence of competence via GCE 'O' and 'A' levels created uncertainties for students on all the courses. In one instance a student who had left school with three 'A's was asked, during an interview, for her grades. The system of grading had been altered in the ten years since she took the examinations, and in her case was by then irrelevant, but it did not stop the interviewers requiring the evidence from the examination board. If the attitudes of a particular institution were quite inflexible and no alternative application was feasible, students were advised to double-up the Fresh Horizons course with correspondence or class-room study for the required GCE. Some succeeded (and while working full-time) in passing, with a few months' preparation, the examinations for which schoolchildren or college of further education students required two years' preparation. Encouragement, counselling and tutorial help always remained available for such students even though their attendance on the part-time courses suffered. In the first year of the full-time course a clash of interests was expected on this score but, in the event, none of the students had cause to need formal entry qualifications —but not without having made many useless and sometimes mortifying applications.

The timing of decisions regarding applications for college or university places created problems. The need for these to be made in the first term, if a start was to be made in the next academic year, created unrest and uncertainty and interrupted the work-flow. This was particularly so for the full-time students, most of whom had entered the course with fairly clearly defined ambitions and who very quickly infected the remaining minority. Studies were interrupted by researches into CRAC guides, *Which University?* and the CNAA handbook. Feverish decision-making problems invaded work-related tutorials: university clearing-house applications had to be made by mid-December; places at colleges of education were filling up by early in the Autumn term; each institution offering social work training had its own procedure and required its own version of evidence of competence. The coming into existence, as time went on, of more CNAA arts and social science courses at polytechnics, with their more flexible admissions policies, was greatly welcomed by students and reduced some of the pressure to make early decisions. This was particularly valuable as the rate of development of students was very variable: some needed more time to find their feet, but in the end surpassed in development others who had got quickly off the mark.

The case with institutions of higher education rested on the evidence of work done and of the capacity shown by the students. The submission of substantial essays, written as part of the Fresh Horizons work, the evidence of reading undertaken and understood, the serious intent of the students themselves, the very careful appraisals of quality and potential made by the tutors that accompanied students' applications and contact with admissions personnel, formally and informally, were the means used to storm the citadel. Over the years these methods succeeded to some extent, but the procedure was always hazardous because of changes in admissions policies or personnel in the various institutions.

There was never enough tutorial or administrative time to carry out a satisfactory sales campaign on behalf of the students. Leaflets about the course seldom got into the right hands; letters, if it was known to whom they should be addressed, did get some replies that formed the basis of a dossier; personal visits would have helped but could rarely be fitted in. Students, as part of their development, were encouraged to make their own approaches direct to college and universities. Because of their undoubted personal qualities they proved to be good sales personnel both for themselves and for those who came after them.

One might easily assume that there would be a danger of students becoming unrealistic in their aspirations in the heady atmosphere of newly aroused ambition engendered by the courses. On the contrary, students were found, with rare exceptions, to be over-modest rather than too confident in their self-assessments. Almost always and sometimes very regretfully, students' final decisions were realistic in relation to their capacities, their circumstances or the external constraints that applied to them. A report, produced more than a decade ago, about a National Extension College–BBC experiment in the teaching of English, includes the comment: 'Adult students are for the most part conscientious, co-operative and, above all, humble. Far from regarding themselves as casualties of an inadequate and ramshackle system, they see themselves as educational failures.'[3] It was well said.

Counselling in the learning situation

Even more than guidance in finding the right routes onwards, Fresh Horizons students, making the plunge into intensive study with no more educational equipment than that gained at school ten, twenty or thirty years earlier and any haphazardly acquired later additions, needed all the reassurance and encouragement that the tutorial staff could give. Tutorial help and counselling of necessity went together and one of the advantages of working within the Fresh Horizons framework was that this was a built-in assumption. It is evident from the facts in Chapter 4, that students often changed their intentions during the course because it gave them opportunity to assess their capacities and interests in the light of their continuing studies. It was a situation that gave time for motives and aspirations to become clearer, for alternatives to be explored and, because it was a context in which growth was taking place, new skills and confidence could be developed. Not the least advantage was that students could decide *not* to embark on new ventures. In meeting the actual demands of intensive study or the more rigorous life required by attendance at the course, they could revise their ambitions and choose less strenuous objectives than they might, at first, have contemplated.

Class meetings also provided opportunities to discuss common difficulties about getting down to work, putting pen to paper seriously and reading with the intent to learn. Tutorial help had, in the first place, to be directed to these ends. The abstract requirements of scholarship, the academic challenge, came later but grew out of the subject material of the course. It was helpful, too, in relation to the changing personal and family circumstances in which students were often caught up that these were frequently reflected in the content of the social studies and English classes. A student excused her late arrival, one morning, by saying, 'I think I'm suffering from role confusion. I can't switch on to my student role till I've chivvied the children to school'. One young man admitted that he had lived through his own Oedipal situation vicariously in *Sons and Lovers* and realized this had been a factor in his choice of a distant college. Identification with *Jude the Obscure* was, of course, rife. The exploration of individual experience in autobiographical and creative writing helped to release emotional tensions left over from the past and to strengthen the awareness of identity.

The counselling standpoint

The experience gained in counselling on the course is re-examined in a wider context in Chapter 10 but a brief indication is desirable here of the assumptions on which practice was based. Discussions with individual students, outside the group, centred on progress being made and any problems arising out of the work of the course, decisions about the future and personal circumstances affecting those decisions. Decisions were wholly matters for the students but the counselling standpoint was not passive. It did not go so far as that of the leaders of the Canadian Centre previously mentioned who say: 'Women seeking to change their lives do not perceive themselves as needing counselling, rather they need information for self-direction'. In the Fresh Horizons situation it was not assumed that students were, necessarily, committed to changing their lives; many of them were on a see-saw of established patterns and tentative aspirations. Information of itself was not enough: neither, on the other hand, was it the right prescription for the student simply to talk out a problem lengthily to a non-directive counsellor, useful as the listening ear can be. Adults have few objective yardsticks for measuring their own abilities. Tutors, knowing the students' developing capacities, could emphasize the points at which they were achieving success and encourage them to have confidence in their abilities. They could recognize, perhaps better than the students themselves, the value of life and work experience as a contribution to any new venture. Sometimes such experience was a starting point in itself, that had been ignored or set aside until looked at from a new angle. Students were most likely to achieve, eventually, what they felt was possible and appropriate if they were encouraged to explore a range of possibilities that could be examined with them in the light of their own capacities, experience and circumstances.

8
Coping

So that Fresh Horizons students should be in no doubt from the outset that the course was serious in intent and demanding of effort, the application form contained the following statement and asked for an endorsement of it: 'A certain amount of prescribed reading and written work at home will be expected of you during this course. Are you willing to do this and are you sure you have the time for it?' After the first two years, perhaps because it was clear that there were a number of prospective students anxious to commit themselves to sustained and organized study, they were told more baldly: 'Reading and written work at home will be expected regularly from you during the course.' Sometimes the applicant's endorsement included a safe-guarding qualification, e.g. 'I see no difficulties in this at present', but always, at the preliminary inferview, further discussion with the tutor left no doubt that the engagement was expected and its implications accepted.

But intentions and assurances have to stand up to experience and the inertia of daily habit: there is always a danger in setting high standards of participation for people caught up in work and family that a conflict of interests can only be resolved by dropping out. Within the tutorial-counselling session students were encouraged to discuss the actual physical or social difficulties that were blocking their efforts. It is hard for a family to realize that the mother is no longer on call, for neighbours and friends not to feel excluded because a mature student refuses invitations to casual outings or for flat-mates to accept that they must turn down the radio when there's an essay to be written. Students had to be helped to see that the importance of what they were doing justified some selfishness and the right to withdraw, but also to find the solutions within the circumstancse of their lives. They had to learn that serious reading was perhaps better tackled in the fore-front of the weekend than after a full day's work at the office; that a house-wife's best time was probably between 10 a.m. and 12 p.m., not 10 p.m. and 12 a.m. and that she should now feel guilty because she was *not* reading poetry instead of because she was not washing the bedroom curtains.

What further adjustments to the daily schedule were possible to make time for study? Would it be better to stay on after classes to read or to escape the calls of friends or the chatter of flat-mates by using the public library? These problems are real ones for mature students. Unlike those in late adolescence, whose whole *raison d'être* is to be students, they must always take into account estab-lished claims and responsibilities. Even the simple matter of escap-ing into the study—if one can be contrived—presents more than physical difficulties; the new role must be made acceptable within established patterns of relationships.

But this is not the whole problem; mature students have uncer-tainties within themselves about their new role both as to their intellectual capacity, as yet untried, and their acceptance as students by society at large. Even young full-time students, firmly estab-lished as such, reinforce their identity by their dress, their scarves, T-shirts, bookbags or whatever is the current signal of their clan, but adult students may be mothers with shopping baskets or fathers with briefcases and, as students, are outside the norms of their own age-groups as well as those of a student body to which they may be nominally attached. They frequently hesitate to reveal themselves to strangers for what they are, too much halting explanation being required, and old friends, left out of these new interests, may feel rejected.

Once having accepted the role, however, mature students have the advantage that they have already explored many of the mysteries of life and living that still perplex their adolescent counterparts. Some may still find themselves in the tumult of a new love affair but the exploration and experimenting that is part of the adolescent learning pattern is already locked in the adult experience.

Test piece

The part-time day course was a testing ground for fresh patterns of living, in which students could gain the acceptance of their families and friends to new assertions about themselves before plunging into full-time work or study. From what they say, this was more difficult than meeting the claims of domestic work, which usually lent itself to reorganization, sometimes after an initial struggle to maintain standards born of a surplus of housewifely pride and time.

To find out how students, their families and friends, had reacted to the new circumstances and what adjustments had been necessary and possible, the following questions were asked:

'What adjustments did you have to make in your normal way of life—job, home and family, social obligations—*to attend the course?*'
'Did you notice any effects *while taking the course* on your:
Home and family relations?
Social relations?
Relations with work associates?'

Only four women on the part-time day course recorded themselves as having difficulty in 'making do' in the house itself. Half of them said that they had adapted their timetables, organized their work more efficiently or let drop some of the more fussy housewifely chores. One of them wrote, 'Stopped doing non-essentials, e.g. ironing drying-up cloths; stopped making lunch for my husband on City Lit days; had people in less often.' Another said, 'Spent less time cooking and shopping; used more convenience foods.' But the old Eve died hard: 'Housework went undone: sometimes I would feel guilty and do the housework instead of studying.' Many housewives recorded no change in their normal habits, evidence of the partial redundancy that had led them to look outside for interest and stimulus.

Husbands and children were more of a worry and in the case of nearly one-quarter of the husbands and for thirty-one of nearly eighty families where there were children, the reduced time available was, at first, felt to present difficulties. But as one student put it, and this applied to many, 'I would not have started the course in the first place if the days and times had been inconvenient to the family.' Of eighteen women affected, ten felt that they had been able to make satisfactory adjustments in relation to husbands and twenty out of thirty-one of them to their children's needs. If there were already strains within the family relationships this was naturally more difficult. Where one student found that the course had given her 'some confidence with which to face a difficult personal relationship', another found she had been hoping for too much from it in that direction:

> 'The children felt I was depriving them when studying while they were at home. Husband resented this non-vocational course. I had attended marriage guidance clinics for some months with no results and wanted to try education as a cure for my personal difficulties. I found these merely made me a poor student, particularly when studying at home.'

Several students said they had found it necessary to curtail visits to elderly relatives and a quarter of the respondents had to make adjustments to their social life and commitments, in order to take the course. 'Until friends realized I was serious about my studies', wrote one, 'it was difficult to stop them from calling and ringing.' Another recorded that she stopped entertaining half-way through the course and told her friends that she wouldn't see them for three months.

On a happier note, nearly half the women found their relations with their families improved during the course and more than a quarter recorded a better harmony in their friendships. Such remarks as the following expressed their satisfaction with this:

> 'The family appeared quite surprised that I could put pen to paper and persevere with study. Friends enjoyed hearing about what happened on the course.'
> 'My son asked more readily for advice on his school work.'
> 'You were looked at as not quite such a cabbage.'
> 'Some friends laughed: others wished they could do the same.'
> 'I had something more interesting than babies and housework to talk about.'

But some negative and adverse effects were noted:

> 'My family approved but regarded it as fairly unimportant.'
> 'My husband resented the time spent in reading and preparation.'

'Began to find some friends awfully misinformed: the sociology aspect of the course did this for me.'
'Hostility from a few friends who felt I had taken on too much and resented that I didn't see them so often.'

Easier by night?

The evening students who reported (and it is well to remember from time to time, those who did not, including those who dropped out) had fewer worries at the outset about the effect of the course on their home and family relationships. If working and married, whether with children (and these were usually older ones) or without, a pattern of adjustment had already been established or could be varied to meet the requirements of the course. 'Housework', said one happily, 'just got neglected': another wrote, 'I had to go to fewer PTA meetings but continued with the swimming club where I was secretary but cut down on church-going.' For the majority, who had no family responsibilities, the chief adjustment was in regard to their jobs. Although two-thirds recorded that they were not so affected, a fifth needed to adjust hours, work later other days, forgo lunch hours and renounce overtime. This was certainly a factor in the drop-out from the evening courses.

Social relations were also, at the outset, affected. Two-thirds of the evening women students felt that relations with friends were either unchanged or satisfactorily adjusted at the outset of the course but the substantial remainder of one-third recorded that it made for loss of contact. As a counter to this, new friends were made during the course, and a third of the respondents reported that, as a result, social relations improved, sometimes with old acquaintances but, within the existential pattern of life of the footloose, mainly with new ones. 'Though lost contact with some friends, saw a lot of people on the course', wrote one. 'Interests broadened, made new friends', wrote another, who also noted 'home relations tense'. Another felt 'An ability to expand, discuss views and ideas, reducing shyness and loss of confidence'.

For some, an improvement in confidence spread to their working situations: 30 per cent of respondents felt that kind of benefit. It could have been a bit difficult for their colleagues! 'I was a bit more bumptious and I think, the better for it—less tolerant of mediocrity' and 'Began to feel slightly superior at work to those to whom before I had felt inferior' are two of the ways in which this change is expressed.

The men on the evening courses mention similar adjustments to jobs. Their replies show a considerable improvement in social relations as a result of the course and almost wholly within it, well over half of them mentioning this. One male student spelt out what others experienced either wholly or in part:

Adjustments to attend the course

Job—gave away my overtime
Housework—neglected
Children—put them out of my mind (he had none!)
Husband or wife—substitute relegated to another world
Elderly relative—retired into the background for a year
Social obligations—cancelled

Effects while taking the course on:

Home and family relations—	they thought I was crazy
Social relations—	they thought I was an egghead
Relations with work associates—	they all thought I was taking a big step towards something
Family, friends and associates—	included in the effects was a certain amount of enigmatic speculation as to the outcome of my schooling; everyone was interested.

It was noticeable, on the evening courses, that the development of a new social environment within the course itself, for whatever reason of mutual attractions and blends of personalities or the charisma of a tutor, helped to retain its initial impetus and the students to enjoy continued mutual support. Contacts and enthusiasm grew in the spontaneous pub sessions at the close of classes and in theatre visits and weekend courses. But sometimes, when the course fortuitously lacked a centre that generated activity, members found it harder to make the effort in work and attendance demanded of them by it. Within the day courses, individual and small-group alliances were made, but the centre of social life and allegiance for most of these students was elsewhere—in their homes or their neighbourhoods. Within the times of course meetings, however, a strong group identity was usually evident.

Impacts of change

The Fresh Horizons students often joined a course because they saw in it a hope of meeting the challenge of a change in their personal circumstances or one dictated by social or economic factors. An enquiry on this was made in the questionnaire:

> Experience has shown that a number of students have been involved in one or more changes in their personal lives and circumstances immediately before or during the course, e.g. moving house, child starting school, a close bereavement, separation or divorce, hospital treatment or operation. If this was the case with you, would you say what the circumstances were, including anything not mentioned above?

Table 19 provides a numerical summary of the replies to this question.

Nearly three-fifths of the women on the day courses mentioned significant changes of circumstances. Those occurring immediately

Table 19 *Respondents—numbers reporting changes of circumstances specified before/during course*

types of change reported	women (Pt-T) day before	during	total	women (Pt-T) evening before	during	total	men (Pt-T) evening before	during	total
N =			105			53			27
illness—self	12	8	20	5	1	6	1	–	1
illness/death/ others	3	8	11	–	2	2	–	–	–
house moves	5	11	16	5	2	7	1	2	3
marriage break	11	5	16	3	2	5	3	–	3
child related	7	2	9	2	–	2	–	–	–
job change	5	3	8	5	3	8	6	1	7
other	3	3	6	5	4	9	1	–	1
numbers of changes	46	40	86	25	14	39	12	3	15
numbers reporting			60			31			9
numbers reporting (%)			(57)			(57)			(33)

before the courses, centred most frequently round marriage break-up and children leaving home or starting school. Where house moves took place, they had usually been planned before the course and embarking on the course often seemed an additional declaration of change. Indeed it sometimes seemed as if there was a Fresh Horizons syndrome, in which changes relating to a husband, a child, a house, or a job, were all possible elements in a new look at oneself. One student described her changing domestic circumstances in these terms: 'Second (last) child started school just before. Major conversion of kitchen/living-room which was to be a panacea became an impossible image. My husband learnt to drive and we bought a car instead of further house improvements.' Another described a series of circumstances that led to a feeling of isolation: 'The course helped me to settle into the change of circumstances of giving up a part-time job I had done for six years as a doctor's receptionist, my daughter (only child) had recently left school and was living away from home for the first time and our family pet, a poodle bitch, had died within the last few weeks.'

Actual marriage break-up, which affected 15 per cent of the day-time respondents, was noticeably a much more commonly accompanying circumstance (and a reason for joining a course) in the last two years of the survey period. There were seven in the first six years and nine in the last two. But dissatisfaction with a marriage or relationship, sometimes leading to actual break-up later, was a contributory reason inclining a number of women to join a course. One referred to, 'the temporary relationship with my boy friend that proved rather complicated and therefore I terminated it because I realized my studies were more important', and another wrote, 'I felt great dissatisfaction about my marriage before and during the course. But I think in some ways, the course made me realize what a complete non-person I had become and gave me a great impetus to think about the importance of developing my own life. I separated from my husband in the following year.'

Just the same proportion of women on the evening as on the day courses—nearly three-fifths—reported relevant changes with a rather different balance of reasons. Marriage break-up was obviously less in evidence in this group of largely single girls. Changes of residence were also perhaps less important but health was still a factor. One married student wrote, 'I had just finished a course of therapy with a psycho-analyst and felt a great need to educate myself—to prove to myself that I was not stupid—also to prepare for a job of some sort.'

Circumstances relating to work were now the most commonly quoted, being twice as important as among the day students. 'Rumours of redundancy' wrote a woman bank-clerk in her late 40s. An administrative assistant at the BBC found that, 'A recent promotion necessitated further educational experience to boost morale and self-confidence to cope with the extra responsibility.' A number totalling up to 17 per cent of these evening student respondents declared a mixed bag of circumstances that included marriage while on the course, the influence of friends and relatives who had made career changes and the realization of the approach of significant ages—30, 40 or 50 as the case might be. The difficulties of women with children under school age attending evening course were shown in the reply of one young mother, 'Baby-sitting arrangements were upset by my husband going into hospital and standing for the Council and my paid baby-sitter being lured away with a colour television set.'

With men the job factor was the most important. Among this much smaller group, seven of the changes reported by men on the evening courses were related to careers. One wrote, 'there had been a change-over in senior officials and management at my place of employment which had displaced my ambitions. During the course and towards the end I decided to resign my job and aim for a new career.'

Commitment—self-assessment

Though many of the changes of circumstances were preliminary to the course, there was usually a continuing effect throughout the session which, together with new changes, affected attendance and concentration. To see how students measured themselves up to the undertakings they had given at the outset, they were asked how they assessed their attendance and work. As regards the first they were asked:

How do *you* regard your own attendance on the course?
Please mark each subject named according to the following scale:
A—Good; B—Good with interruption; C—Fair; D—Poor; E—Uncompleted. (If B, C, D or E say why.)

The replies are summarized numerically in Table 20.

Table 20   *Respondents—class attendance—self-assessment*

subject	women—Pt-T day N = 105						men—Pt-T day N = 7					
	% giving self-rating						giving self-rating					
	A %	B %	C %	D %	E %	none %	A (N)	B (N)	C (N)	D (N)	E (N)	none (N)
English Literature	65	25	1	–	7	2	(4)	(2)	(1)	–	–	–
English Language	64	24	3	–	6	3	(4)	(3)	–	–	–	–
Social Study	55	29	6	1	8	1	(4)	(1)	(2)	–	–	–
Speech and Drama	53	20	6	8	10	3	(2)	–	–	(2)	(3)	–
Tutorial	56	27	3	1	7	6	(2)	(1)	(1)	–	–	(3)
Mathematics	46	23	5	6	14	6	(2)	–	–	(1)	(2)	(2)
	women—evening N = 53						men—evening N = 27					
	%	%	%	%	%	%	(N)	(N)	(N)	(N)	(N)	(N)
English Literature	67	21	4	–	8	–	(25)	(1)	(1)	–	–	–
English Language	61	22	4	–	9	4	(25)	(2)	–	–	–	–
Social Study	50	28	4	4	9	5	(16)	(4)	(4)	(1)	(2)	–
Speech and Drama	42	20	4	17	11	6	(16)	(9)	(1)	(1)	–	–

Attendance records of students are more fully analysed in Chapter 9, but it is interesting to note here that attendance by subjects, as assessed by students themselves, shows the same order of precedence as is recorded in the registers. The proportionate popularity of subjects as represented by the replies and records of those responding to the questionnaire is very close to the ranking of attendances for all registered students, which encourages a belief in the capacity of the respondents to assess themselves objectively.

Students were asked similar questions as regards work done on the course, i.e.:

How do you regard your own record of work done on the course as regards:
Reading of set books?
Additional reading and research?
Written work?
Preparation of material for presentation in class?
Please grade according to the following scale
A—a lot; B—a fair amount; C—inadequate; D—much too little (If B, C or D, say why.)

Table 21 *Respondents—work done on course—self-assessment*

| type of work | women—Pt-T day N = 105 | | | | | men—Pt-T day N = 7 | | | | |
| | % giving self-rating | | | | | giving self-rating | | | | |
	A %	B %	C %	D %	none %	A (N)	B (N)	C (N)	D (N)	none (N)
reading set books	49	38	9	1	3	(2)	(2)	–	(3)	–
additional reading	15	47	24	7	7	–	(1)	(2)	(4)	–
written work	38	35	19	3	5	–	(3)	(2)	(2)	–
preparation for class presentation	36	40	12	8	4	(1)	(1)	(2)	(3)	–
	women—evening N = 53					men—evening N = 27				
	%	%	%	%	%	(N)	(N)	(N)	(N)	(N)
reading set books	32	47	19	2	–	(6)	(14)	(5)	(2)	–
additional reading	13	34	30	23	–	(5)	(13)	(4)	(4)	(1)
written work	11	59	20	8	2	(6)	(9)	(9)	(3)	–
preparation for class presentation	15	43	17	15	10	(10)	(7)	(8)	(1)	(1)

The replies summarized in Table 21 reveal the greater pressure on the evening students. More of them, relatively, record their work on the essentials of reading set books and providing written work as inadequate. Taking ratings A and B together ('a lot' and 'a fair amount') they were not far below the level of the day students but this relative parity is achieved by the much larger percentages of evening students according themselves the second level rating.

Employment obstacles

It is relevant to the question of 'coping' to note that no student in these eight years was released from work—given 'paid educational leave', in the current terminology—to attend a part-time day course. Some day-time students gave up work temporarily and lived on savings—one on a premium bond win—to concentrate on study, or fitted temporary part-time shift work around the two days of the course. A handful of evening students were able to recoup their very modest fees from their employing bodies but none was given time off for study. Very rarely was there any sign from employers that benefit might accrue to them from having better-informed and better-educated employees. It is true that most evening students were looking at the possibilities of career change as a direct outcome of dissatisfaction with their present jobs. Their record of achievement on the courses, and subsequently, shows that many of them, at least, were right in their judgments of their own capacities.

Employers were at fault, first, in not recognizing the potential of their staff and second, in not encouraging their further education. The setting-up of the full-time course in 1973, accompanied by the availability of student maintenance grants, encouraged disgruntled employees to resign and make a clear break with their jobs. Given the chance of day-release for part-time study with prospects of promotion attached, some of the students might have preferred to stay with their existing employers. But they were still compelled to study under all the pressures associated with 'night-school'— pressures that are reflected in the evening students' own assessments of their course work and attendance. Even so, what many of them achieved, under the limitations to which both they and their tutors were subject, was often remarkable. Records of written work and reading undertaken are incomplete, but the following reports from students are reasonably representative of the scope and character of the work expected from students and achieved by the majority over the years.

Evening students—records of a term's work—three examples

I

ENGLISH, SPOKEN AND WRITTEN

Short essay on 'Care of old people'	Completed
Short essay on 'Christmas presents'	Completed
Summary of 'The use of poetry and the use of criticism'	Completed

ENGLISH LITERATURE

Summary on 'The origins of *Othello*'	Completed
Individual essay on 'The condition of the Moors in the 17th century'	Nearly completed— will be handed in

Extended essay on an aspect of
   D. H. Lawrence's work   Not completed—
                                   still working on it

SOCIOLOGY
Essay on 'Education and social background'   Not completed—
                                   but will make an
                                   attempt before
                                   end of term

SPEECH AND DRAMA
Project—individual piece written by myself

2

ENGLISH, SPOKEN AND WRITTEN
Three essays
One précis
Criticism of poem—in class

ENGLISH LITERATURE
One précis
Study in essay form of Witchcraft
Essay on difference between Joyce and Lawrence

SOCIAL STUDIES
Essay—Relationship between individual and society

DRAMA AND SPEECH
Investigation into poetry—facts and quotations

3

ENGLISH LITERATURE
Summary of Prefatory remarks in the Signet *Othello*
Summarize the sources of *Othello*
Discuss the view that the world of *Othello* is evil
(Missed work comparing D. H. Lawrence in 1913 with his
   views in 1929)
Comparing descriptive passage in *The Rainbow*, male and
   female characteristics

SOCIAL STUDIES
Extended essay about the 1944 Education Act

SPEECH AND DRAMA
Preparation of 'documentary' on coal-mining: wrote script for
a school lesson on the history of coal in preparation for a
visit to a coal-mine
Found advertisement for apprentice miners to use as conclusion
Typed chart showing layout of the programme
Obtained booklet from Educational Publications Ltd

ENGLISH, SPOKEN AND WRITTEN
Art criticism
Summary of T. S. Eliot's views on poetry
Class essay—'Censorship and morals'
Report on 'Any Questions'
Summary of passage from *Erewhon*
Exercise in the use of personal pronouns
Comments upon 'Anthem for Doomed Youth', by Wilfred Owen
Class essay, 'My job'

Day students—two examples of reading and written work programmes

I

SOCIAL STUDIES

Books read:	Author
The Year of Freedom	E. Fromm
Anatomy of Britain	Anthony Sampson
Introduction to Marxism	Emile Burns
The Social Psychology of Industry	J. A. C. Brown
Report of the Committee on Maladjusted Children	Min. of Education
The Social Structure of Modern Britain	E. H. Johns
The New Class	Milovan Djilas
Books partly read:	
Sense and Non-sense in Psychology	H. J. Eysenck
Liberal Studies I	Blackman
An Introduction to Logic	M. Cohen and E. Nagel
The Affluent Society	J. K. Galbraith

MATHEMATICS
Books partly studied:

The New Mathematics	Irving Adler
Mathematicians' Delight	W. W. Sawyer
First Course in Statistics	R. Loveday
The Use and Abuse of Statistics	W. K. Reichman
Facts from Figures	M. J. Morony

LITERATURE
Set books:

Macbeth	Shakespeare
Daniel Deronda	George Eliot
The Penguin Book of English Verse	
The Tempest	Shakespeare

Books read in connection with these:

Introducing Shakespeare	G. B. Harrison
An Approach to Shakespeare	P. A. Traversi
The Tragedy of Macbeth	J. R. Brown
Pelican History of England 5. Tudor	S. T. Bindoff

Biography of George Eliot
Cymbeline
The Winter's Tale }—in connection with
Pericles }   *The Tempest*
The Metaphysical Poets (parts)

ENGLISH SOCIAL STUDIES

Lark Rise to Candleford	Flora Thomson
North Country Bred	Stella Davies
Early English Lyric Poetry	

2

Preparation of two chosen pieces for 'Speech and Drama'.
  Extract from *Catch 22* and 'Shall I compare thee to a
  Summer's day?'
Choice of music for 'How beautiful is the night'—Speech and
  Drama
Essay on 'The Apparition' by John Donne
Paraphrase speech from *King Lear* and give reasons for thinking
  it important—Literature

Compare 'Ode to the West Wind' by Shelley and 'Autumn' by Keats

Write essay 'British family life isn't what it used to be'. Discuss this statement with regard to *Cider with Rosie*—Sociology

(Individual work) Summarize *Child Care and the Growth of Love* by Dr John Bowlby—Sociology

Précis *Erewhon*—Spoken and Written English

Give permutations on 'John told Robert's son', etc.

'Anthem for doomed youth'—imagery and opinion of poem

Preparation of questionnaire to colleges of education—summarize replies (work not yet completed)

Struggle on desperately to keep with the Maths class (Work will never be completed)

9
Those who got away

The demands made on students in the Fresh Horizons courses for class attendance and work to be done at home are larger than is usual in part-time non-certificate adult education. Some of the motives and resistances that served as spurs and deterrents to effort have already been indicated. It was only to be expected that, in some cases, there was initial misapprehension of the extent of effort demanded or that it would prove more difficult to sustain as the course went on.

The questionnaire that was used to get information and opinions from students was sent only to those who could be regarded as having substantially completed the attendance they undertook to make. Only those, it was felt, would be able to make the very detailed appraisal of the course and its effects that was sought. They included, however, a very few students who made a diminished attendance but had a continuing relationship with the class for tutorial help and counselling because they were additionally working for 'A' levels, by correspondence or otherwise, to satisfy entry requirements that universities would not waive.

The full-time students are not considered in this chapter. The circumstances under which they were attending their course put them, in general, into a separate category. As regards attendance they all, with the exception of one woman who, at a late stage, withdrew because she said she could not afford to refuse the offer of an enhanced salary, completed the course satisfactorily.

The questionnaire was therefore sent to 294 out of 388 part-time students, 70 per cent of those whose names were included on the permanent registers of the classes. The response from 192 represented 65 per cent of those approached and 49 per cent of the total number of registered students. The response rate was uneven as between day and evening students, being 77 per cent for the former and 54 per cent for the latter.

For the students who did not reply (designated 'N') and for those who were not approached because of low or withdrawn attendance (designated 'NA'), there is information derived from their application forms, supplemented by correspondence and notes made during personal and class contacts with them. The basic information covers age, occupation, previous occupation, previous education (including any examinations passed and adult education classes attended). In most cases the marital status of the women was known and there is no obvious difference in the proportions of married, single, married formerly, as between respondents and non-respondents, except perhaps among women registered for the day courses where single women comprise 14 per cent of the 'N's and 'NA's, as against 9 per cent of the respondents. In no other element of background information is there any defining difference between respondents and non-respondents whether male or female.

The non-respondents ('N's) are, however, revealed as having on the whole a poorer record of attendance on the courses, while the 'NA's, by definition, withdrew from the course. In trying to establish a scale by which effective attendance on the courses could be measured, two approaches were made. In the first (A), the total possible attendances for each course were calculated, being the number of weeks of the course multiplied by the number of hours to be attended each week. For students joining the course after the first week, separate possible attendance hours were calculated according to the number of weeks remaining in the session at the time of their enrolment. Students making two-thirds or more of the personally possible attendances were deemed to have been 'Fully effective' attenders and were designated S1. Those making between one-third and two-thirds of their possible attendances were designated S2 and classed as 'Effective but limited' attenders. The remainder, with less than one-third of possible attendances, were designated S3 indicating 'Less than adequate attendance for effective participation'.

Scale (B) took this basic classification as the starting point for the examination of each student's actual attendances, with a special eye to people on the border-lines of the respective categories. A student whose attendance ended completely at a late point in the course was not necessarily put into a lower category. Frequently such withdrawals were a product of the course itself, e.g. the approach of a GCE examination or a student returning, after domesticity, to outside employment. Absences might also be due to authentic illness, the demands of shift work and the plague of public service strikes and withdrawals that characterized several years of the period here surveyed.[1]

Table 22 *Effectiveness of attendance of all part-time students—comparison of two scales and analysis of one by sex*

| | scale A | | | scale B | | | | | | | | |
| | all | | | all | | | women | | | men | | |
	S1	S2	S3	S1	S2	S3	S1	S2	S3	S1	S2	S3
day students —all years												
N =	100	52	36	112	37	39	103	35	30	9	2	9
% =	(53)	(28)	(19)	(60)	(20)	(20)	(61)	(21)	(18)	(45)	(10)	(45)
evening students —all years												
N =	101	64	35	110	39	51	74	24	44	35	15	7
% =	(51)	(32)	(17)	(55)	(19)	(26)	(52)	(17)	(31)	(62)	(26)	(12)

On the other hand, some students who otherwise had a good record of attendance throughout the course, ceased to attend for a component subject at some stage, and this was taken into account: since the course was entered into as a package deal, students might be put in a lower category than a simple summation of their attendances would have merited. Table 22 also extends the Scale B assessment to distinguish between men and women. The small group of day-time men were clearly less committed than their evening counterparts, whilst the greater obstacles to attendance faced by women on the evening courses as compared with those on the day courses are clearly evident.

Enrolled but unregistered

The number of registered students excludes people who enrolled but left a course within the first three weeks of the first term, this being the point at which names are transferred from temporary to permanent registers. There were twenty-eight such people on the eight day courses (twenty women and eight men), and twenty-nine (eighteen women and eleven men) on the six evening ones. This total of fifty-seven people comprises 13 per cent of the 445 who completed application forms. Because they did this, some information is available about them and some of them also gave or indicated reasons for their early withdrawal from the course. It is not uncommon for students to use the three weeks' grace of the temporary register to try out a course's suitability to their purposes and to transfer to another if it does not meet their expectations. For the Fresh Horizons courses, it was the practice during initial interviews to present as clear a picture as possible of what membership would entail and, though in some cases alternative courses were suggested by the enrolling tutor, some people did not fully grasp just how intensive or demanding the course would be. Some simply found it too hard, some decided to do 'O' and 'A' levels instead, others, e.g. nurses, had difficulty in adjusting working hours to regular attendance. Other opportunities were sometimes being explored concurrently and sometimes the decision to join a course was a spur, in itself, to other independent action, e.g. 'I am withdrawing my application because I have been offered a part-time post in connection with becoming a health visitor which is what I was aiming for eventually.' After describing various offers of jobs that had appeared once she had started looking for new outlets, one woman wrote,

> 'I think in some curious way the mere fact that I galvanized myself into action to start the Fresh Horizons course, acted as a sort of spring-board for all these other things I have got involved in. But I think, regretfully, I will not be coming back not because I didn't find it interesting—I did—but I've got involved in so many other things now that I don't think I'll have the time! One thing I am quite sure of though, and that is if I hadn't started with you I would not have started anything. I owe you a big "thank you" for having jerked me out of my mole-like existence.'

Difficulties could occur at the start of a session, with last-minute applications released by a late item of publicity. Though many applicants found a useful answer to their felt needs, others rushed in with too little consideration of the adjustments they would have to make. The class grew in size and became unwieldy while decisions about splitting it were pending. In one instance while this was happening a man wrote, 'I'm sorry I cannot continue with the Fresh Horizons course. I was a bit overwhelmed by the large class. Ten or a dozen I may have been able to manage (fifteen was the minimum average required by the authority). I shall attempt a correspondence course instead.'

Recruitment early in the summer became the practice, as the courses were more widely known. This helped to prevent hasty decisions that led to early drop-out. But the mid-September enrolment period continued to bring in applicants whose needs could not be denied even though their presence created problems for the small staff working with limited resources.

Reasons given

Many students volunteered reasons for absence or for leaving the course and no one dropped out without receiving at least two letters from the tutor-in-charge, seeking reasons for non-attendance. Reasons given, however, may be excuses to cover dissatisfactions with the course itself which are tactfully glossed over. Tutors may, indeed, become unduly sensitized to what they may feel to be the implied criticism in the act of withdrawal which may, after all, be due simply to the total demands that life presents to part-time students. Tables 23 and 24 summarize what is known of reasons for withdrawal from an examination of the registers of attendance and the students' individual records. Altogether, more than half the withdrawals are reasonably accounted for. The following statements typify three of the main reasons for withdrawal—over-commitment, qualification seeking and under-assessment of difficulties.

'You may remember that you kindly discussed the fact that I was doing rather a lot of things study-wise and you suggested that I should try to think of myself as taking the full-time FH course. I have tried to do this but I find I seem to be so

Table 23 *Part-time day students enrolled and entered on permanent registers—yearly attendances and withdrawals*

	D66		D67		D68		D69		D70		D71		D72		D73		all courses		
	W	M	W	M	W	M	W	M	W	M	W	M	W	M	W	M	W	M	T
1. Withdrew week 1–3 (not entered on register)	2	2	1	1	2	—	2	—	3	2	4	2	5	—	1	1	20	8	28
2. On permanent register	15	2	25	4	19	1	18	4	20	2	28	2	24	—	22	5	171	20	191*
3. Withdrew by mid-first term	1	1	2	—	—	—	—	—	1	—	2	—	—	—	2	1	8	2	10
4. Withdrew by end first term	3	—	5	1	—	—	1	3	3	—	3	1	2	—	2	—	19	5	24
5. Withdrew by mid-second term	—	—	1	2	—	—	—	—	3	1	6	—	—	—	—	—	10	3	13
6. Partial withdrawal	2	—	1	—	2	—	—	—	—	—	—	—	—	—	—	—	5	—	5
7. Total withdrawal	6	1	9	3	2	—	1	3	7	1	11	1	2	—	4	1	42	10	52
8. Number on permanent register completing the course	9	1	16	1	17	1	17	1	13	1	17	1	22	—	18	4	129	10	139
9. Line 8 as per cent of line 2	60%	50%	64%	25%	89%	100%	94%	25%	65%	50%	61%	50%	92%	—	82%	80%	75%	50%	71%

*This figure differs by 3 from the analysis of day students in Table 22 because of transfers between day and evening courses leading to double registrations.

Table 24 *Evening students enrolled and entered on permanent registers—yearly attendances and withdrawals*

	E68		E69		E70		E71		E72		E73		all courses		
	W	M	W	M	W	M	W	M	W	M	W	M	W	M	T
1. Withdrew weeks 1–3—not entered on permanent registers	4	1	–	2	7	3	3	–	3	3	2	1	19	10	29
2. On permanent registers	26	10	22	16	22	12	32	9	16	7	24	4	142	58	200
3. Withdrew by mid-first term	1	–	3	2	–	1	5	1	2	–	4	–	15	4	19
4. Withdrew by end first term	4	–	1	2	5	–	6	2	1	–	4	–	21	4	25
5. Withdrew by mid-second term	–	–	2	1	–	–	–	–	–	1	1	1	3	3	7
6. Partial withdrawal	3	1	1	–	–	–	3	–	1	–	–	–	8	1	9
7. Total withdrawal	8	1	7	5	5	1	14	3	4	1	9	1	47	12	59
8. Numbers on permanent registers completing course	18	9	15	11	17	11	18	6	12	6	15	3	95	46	141
9. Line 8 as per cent of line 2	69%	90%	68%	69%	77%	92%	57%	67%	75%	86%	63%	75%	67%	78%	70%

Table 25 *Part-time day students—reasons for withdrawals so far as known*

	withdrawals			reasons									remarks
courses	applica- tions	weeks 1–3	later	work	left London	own illness	illness others	other reasons known	not known				
	W M	W M	W M	W M	W M	W M	W M	W M	W M				
D66	17 4	2 2	6 —	— —	— —	— —	— —	— —	2 2				
D67	26 5	1 1	9 3	1 —	— —	— —	2 —	2 —	2 1				
D68	21 1	2 —	2 —	2 1	— —	— —	— —	2 —	— 2				course unsuitable (1); too old to train (1)
D69	20 4	2 —	1 3	1 1	1 —	1 —	— —	1 —	— 2				'A' levels (1)
D70	23 4	3 2	7 1	1 —	3 1	1 1	— —	1 —	2 1				marriage (1)
D71	32 4	4 2	11 1	1 —	3 1	1 —	1 1	2 1	2 1				class too large (1); too difficult (1)
D72	29 —	5 —	2 —	1 —	— —	2 —	— 1	2 1	— 1				'A' levels (1); too difficult (1)
D73	23 6	1 1	4 (1T) 1 (1T)	2 —	— —	3 —	1 —	4 —	3 1				too difficult (1) / social duties (2) / other course (1)
totals	191 28	20 8	42 (1T) 10 (1T)	9 2	7 2	8 1	4 —	16 3	18 10				

Table 26 *Evening students—reasons for withdrawals so far as known*

courses	applications W	applications M	withdrawals weeks 1-3 W	weeks 1-3 M	later W	later M	work W	work M	left London W	left London M	own W	own M	illness others W	illness others M	other reasons W	other reasons M	not known W	not known M	remarks
E68	30	11	4	1	8	1	1	1	1		2				1		3	1	
E69	22	18		2	7	5			2				1		3	1	3		children (1); marriage (1); too many students (1); tutor (1)
E70	29	15	7	3	5	1			1						3	2	3		too demanding (2); personal (1); floater (1); 'O' level alt. (1)
E71	35	9	3	1	14	3		1	2	1	1			1	1	1	11	3	course too advanced/demanding (1) 'O' level alt. (1) too demanding (1); Open University (1); pregnancy (1) 'O' level alt. (1)
E72	19	10	3	3	4	1	1		1						3		1	1	aged parent (1); 'O' levels (1); Open University (1)
E73	26	5	2		9	1	1	1	1		1	1			2	1	6	2	transport (1); children (1)
totals	161	68	19	10	47	12	3	3	8	1	4	1	1	1	13	5	36	10	

behind with the reading, which I am slow at, and the essays,
that I ought to concentrate on the Drama Diploma
(part-time) and my music theory, both of which I have
homework for and stop the City Lit course. I think I took too
much on, thinking I could do them all, and seem not to be
doing justice to any of them. Thank you so much for your
help and understanding. This has been difficult to decide on
to get my priorities right and I hope I have made the right
decision.'

> (Woman aged 45, on part-time day course. She had origin-
> ally wished to join the full-time course wanting to teach
> Drama having had substantial amateur and professional
> experience)

'Although I found the course interesting I think that one of
my main problems was that I was not studying for any
specific exams and so began to doubt the usefulness of the
course. Also I did not have any firm idea regarding what I
should do at the end of the course which I think affected my
motivation and determination to continue studying. At the
present moment I am considering trying for a few 'O' levels.
I would like to do a Nurse-Tutor's course and five 'O' levels
are required before being accepted by the College.'

> (Man, aged 25 on evening course: a staff-nurse in a mental
> hospital)

'At this particular time in my life, I do not feel capable either
mentally or physically of tackling the course which would
demand my complete concentration. May I add that from my
brief glimpse of the course, I was most impressed with the
members of the class, the informality and the work content.'

> (Woman aged 26, on evening course: no exams at school)

Inadequacy and unease

It was difficult to cater adequately for students with basic literacy
deficiences, particularly men. It was fairly clear from the description of the course that, although there were no set standards for
entry, a degree of elementary scholastic competence was called foɪ.
Some highly motivated students who, on the face of it, had less
than this, made outstanding and consistent efforts to develop the

skills needed to express their expanding range of thought. Some found unsuspected fluency when their imaginations or memories were released. But others, still smarting under a sense of defeat, rejection or inadequacy, were impatient for the help they felt was denied them. Remedial tutoring, if it could have been administered before discontent became established, might have prevented some drop-outs. But when such students—and we had no more than half-a-dozen, the majority men—were coming up against the facts of their basic non-literacy, there was inevitable disappointment.

Any suspicion that those who withdrew in the first three weeks, particularly the men, were characteristically in this category of near-illiteracy is dispelled by a close look at their records. They are too varied in their occupations, origins and early education to be easily distinguishable from those who stayed the course. To some extent they seem to have been seeking a niche without yet being ready to occupy it, ex-merchant navy, ex-army, ex-progressive boarding schools and some social drop-outs not yet completely ready to drop-in. There were some, certainly—salesmen and lorry drivers were examples—who were being pressurized by better-educated wives, to take their education in hand. But counterparts to most of them could be found among the 'settled' students: it may be that something very much more open and casual than even the most informal classroom situation is necessary to provide at least a temporary alighting place for such birds of passage until they are ready for the rigours of the tougher journey. There is no effortless way to learning but it should be possible to 'drop-in' at many different points and to take sightings on many different goals so that learning skills may develop with certainty of will and purpose.

It needs to be said with some force, however, that concern for those who are hard to catch, should not make us deny or disparage the claims of those who have recognized a need and are trying to satisfy it. It is now twenty years since the Crowther Report specified, 'girls and unskilled boys' as losers in the 15-to-19 education stakes, recognizing one class of deprivation as sex- and not class-linked. Confusion in the minds of some ardent protagonists of the need for workers' education, leads them almost to abuse the presence of 'middle-class' women as the prime respondents to offers of adult education, without considering how much their potential growth might have been stunted by a curtailment of educational and training opportunity. Some of the men on Fresh Horizons courses were obviously discomfited to find themselves among more articulate and knowledgeable women. It was a factor in their refusal to stay with the course and one that they could, sometimes, more comfortably attribute to their feelings of class deprivation than to their sex prejudice: students of maturer mind could accept and enjoy the challenge.

Publicity problems

The take-up of publicity for the courses, by press and radio, helped to sway the recruitment for individual courses and brought its own particular benefits and hazards. Students for the first course, according to the questionnaire responses, came in through having seen the widely circulated City Lit prospectus. For the second year, a round-up of information about adult education opportunities in the women's pages of *The Times* and *Daily Telegraph* in mid-September, alerted a number of readers to the existence of the course. The resulting late applicants, when the course was already starting, were a welcomed embarrassment. A parallel course had to be set up in haste, with little opportunity for consideration by either tutors or applicants of the full implications of the undertaking. As a consequence, of thirty-three who applied, two withdrew their applications before the course started, two left before the permanent register was compiled and eight within the first term. But the seventeen students who substantially completed the course are known to have included at least four who went on to colleges of education, one who took a post-graduate diploma course (though not a graduate), one who was ultimately accepted for the Certificate for Qualification in Social Work and two who took work as school librarians. Another of this group of students, while continuing in her job, continued her educational efforts as an Open University student and a second secured a University Extension Diploma in Literature. A more varied but similarly swollen influx, in 1971, resulted from a late article in *Nova* and a mention on the radio, with a somewhat similar outcome for the course.

Mention has been made of variable responses to different tutors and subjects. Where a subject was likely to meet with very mixed degrees of response and the class came into the hands of a tutor who could not generate sufficient enthusiasm to overcome some part of the resistance, unpopularity could overflow and affect attendance at other classes on the same day. It is fair to say that the effects of such failures were marginal and, on enquiry at the time, a dissatisfied client could always be matched with a satisfied one.

10

A counselling service in adult education

The 'winds of change' of an earlier chapter would be reason enough for reverting to the importance of educational counselling even if it were not a current topic of acute concern and active debate. This chapter relates experience derived from Fresh Horizons courses to our own long-held views about the needs for counselling both inside a learning experience and as a major element in educational information and advice services for adults.[1] Many of the Fresh Horizons students belonged to the minority of adults who regularly go to evening classes and, to that extent, were more likely than most people to know what educational possibilities were available. Yet more than half—54 per cent—of the total questionnaire respondents endorsed the statement that the counselling on the course made them aware of possibilities they had not known of. Almost the same proportion confirmed that they were made aware of possibilities that they did not at first think applied to themselves. The emphatic endorsement of the respondents to the statement 'It was an essential part of the course' (69 per cent) completely justified its inclusion as a course element.

Nor was help wholly directed to exploring problems relating to education. Nearly a quarter of the students felt that they were helped 'to sort out personal problems rationally', though this was a derivative from the main scope of the counselling, but an inevitable one in a situation where personal reassessment was taking place.

The need for a counselling service, in this case not directly related to a continuous learning situation, was borne out by a further experience. Under the title of 'Opportunities for Adults' a Saturday

School was mounted at the Richmond Adult College at what was regarded as a substantial fee for participants in a one-day event. The morning session was devoted to talks about new degree courses, the Open University, and the Training Opportunities Scheme of the Manpower Commission. In the afternoon a panel of speakers drawn from the college staff, with the help of the careers officer of the education authority, answered questions on education and career opportunities and discussed some of the problems of adults returning to learning. The fee included the possibility of an individual interview at a later date to discuss the personal relevance of the information and guidance given. Here the reasons emerged why the opportunity created by the school had been seized: the need to find a new angle on life after a marriage break-up or when the last child had started school; the awareness of educational deficiency in the light of current employment or family demands; a sense of unfulfilled ambition and unused ability; the need for personal adjustment to handicap or employment loss. Close on one hundred attended the day school and almost all of them came for a counselling interview. There was a continuing need for further exploration of the problems raised and the suggestions made in the course of the interviews but there was no money available for this within the Adult College budget.

Sources of need

It is not surprising that once help of this kind is offered it is seized upon. In this account of adult education students the extent to which they have been disadvantaged by social and educational change has been emphasized even though they were, on the whole, better equipped than many of their contemporaries to meet it. But because they are better equipped they are all the more likely to be aware of what they are lacking and to seek a remedy when one is offered. There is little enough help readily available for such as these: for those with meagre knowledge from the start, opportunities need to be made manifest.

There are many possible moments of crisis in adult life, at work, in the home, in social life, that trigger off feelings of inadequacy arising from early educational loss, or today's mounting educational expectations. But they do not call merely for routine information and advice. Deep personal attitudes and feelings are involved, differing from person to person.

The survey of Fresh Horizons' students' early education revealed that the older ones were born of parents still smarting under the deprivations of the depression years, anxious above all to see their children into jobs as early and as secure as possible. Men in their 50s were part of the adolescent workforce in the war years, called up for the services or liable to be so during the formative years of their lives, without the benefit of either the pre-war or the post-war opportunities for further education and training. Redundancies and job changes affecting men in their 40s reveal, to this now middle-aged group, the extent to which they are facing the keener competition of the better-educated young. The probability that our total national endeavour has been affected by failure to tackle the basic educational deprivation of the middle-aged band in our present work and management personnel, does not appear to have received much attention from educational sociologists. It was, for example, a matter of some surprise to the Open University's research team, when analysing the characteristics of the first year's student intake, that so many of those in administration and management jobs were early leavers.[2] This was because they were characteristically older than the typical technical and research staffs who had benefited from more recent longer schooling and wider access to further education. Perhaps the effect has been too successfully masked by the achievements of many of the men and women concerned in surmounting their difficulties from a base of relative inadequacy or covered up by the resort to contrivance and expediency.

The post-war generations of schoolchildren have also felt the impact of demographic and social change. Successive birth-rate bulges filled classes to overflowing, teachers came and went and youngsters struggled through or became lost or indifferent. There is, in fact, overwhelming evidence to support the claim that help should be readily available to adults recognizing an educational deprivation, especially when the recognition is heightened by a personal crisis or dilemma, and this is now coming to be more widely accepted and promoted. Reviewing the discussions that came out of a large conference of experienced adult educationists, in 1975, the commentator noted:

Another recurring point concerned the need for a counselling service and the close link between vocational and educational guidance on the one hand and the process of adult education on the other. It also became clear that in the opinion of many, the counselling role is so intimately tied up with the teaching role that no separate guidance system could suffice, but rather, the guidance function has to be expressed in the basic professional skills of adult educators.[3]

These views were strongly represented in the report of the OU Committee on Continuing Education issued in interim and final forms in 1976 but it is strange that the Russell Committee, which should have given a lead, was curiously stiff-necked about counselling needs. Its Report contained only two references to counselling and although the index gives it a heading, it omits the references! It includes 'counselling and the clarification of choices' as one of the necessities for achieving 'the goal of equality of educational opportunity' and continues 'There are two related needs here: for information about the range of educational opportunities provided and for help to an individual in assessing his own objectives and capacities in relation to those opportunities.' So far, so good. But in discussing the provision that needs to be made to implement this the Report says later:

> Equally important is the provision of information to the individual enquirer . . . Help of this kind to enable the individual to identify and locate the most suitable activity for his educational needs is an essential component of a comprehensive service in adult education . . . such action is sometimes referred to as counselling. We believe that the term is better reserved for the full guidance services that are being developed in other sectors of education. These, which use trained counsellors and accepted diagnostic approaches, are distinct from the information services that we are here considering. To establish a true counselling service for adult education would be a costly and elaborate undertaking with heavy training demands, for inexpert counselling is potentially harmful.[4]

More than information

'Provision of information to the individual enquirer' presupposes that the enquirer knows what is needed, and that what is needed exists and that there is a discernible route to it. It might be so if our educational provision were like a railway system instead of, for most people, an uncharted jungle. And even the railway traveller could complain that she 'wanted to go to Birmingham but they sent me on to Crewe'. Enough description of the Fresh Horizons students has been given and analyzed for there to be no doubt that adults seeking a way into remedial or renewal education (or to many other aspects of education) are likely to be shy, lacking in confidence and uncertain of what they are really looking for.

How 'to locate the most suitable activity for his educational needs' can be as little as a bland waving of the prospectus, a skilled interview, or a sympathetic hearing during which the listener's antennae pick up signals of distress. At what point does the non-counsellor stop? And what should he or she do at that point? 'An opportunity for the individual enquirer to clarify for himself through discussion with someone informed about all possibilities', leaves out the possibilities that lie within the enquirer himself. They cannot be omitted and it is these that are 'vital to be recognized'.

Counselling is a continuous process as a new recruit to learning expands under the influence of developing skills. It thrives best in the atmosphere of learning. The student then dares to ask the question, knows more clearly what to ask, probes a variety of possibilities with the counsellor and becomes ripe to make a decision. The counsellor follows the exploration, encouraging the process of self-diagnosis. But whether the process is within the learning situation or not the need exists for more than information to be forthcoming. And if counselling needs have been identified within the university and school system how much more are they likely to exist within a heterogeneous adult population?

Analysis or development

It is customary for counselling professions to distinguish between directive and non-directive counselling, with the latter receiving authority derived from the analyst's consulting room. Indeed, the Russell Committee's caution may have been induced by claims made on behalf of counselling services using techniques deriving from psycho-analysis in which problems are seen as having, almost always, deep-seated emotional origins rather than arising, as they do for the most part in adult education, from historical accident. The point is made by Newsome, Thorne and Wyld that 'Counselling is not psycho-analysis . . . Counsellors need to be clear that their main area of concern will be with people experiencing normal developmental difficulties, together with only a small number who are undergoing moderate or even severe personal problems.'[5] They conclude that the analyst's training is 'ill-suited to a concept of counselling . . . where the emphasis is on developmental needs.' Blocher describes developmental counselling as having 'developmental-educative-preventive goals as opposed to remediative-adjustment-therapeutic outcomes', and as being 'educational in orientation . . . aiming at facilitating human learning of a deeply personal nature'. The counsellor is then 'a helping person, a teacher, a consultant and a confidant'.[6]

In the context of adult education one might go further and describe the process through which adults are being helped to develop new ideas about their capacities and about themselves, in a changing situation, as exploratory counselling—a partnership of counsellor and counselled.

It may be that the Russell Committee was warned off much-disputed and potentially expensive ground when considering counselling needs. Vaughan calls into question the movement in Britain, following Carl Rogers in the USA, 'towards non-directional approaches in existing concepts of guidance' and sees a danger of counselling in Britain becoming 'institutionalized'.[7] The fear of an elaborate counselling service with all the paraphernalia of a professional expertise expensively acquired and exercising a closed shop is understandable. But the alternative is not 'potentially dangerous', nor need it be 'inexpert', as claimed in the Russell Report. It is more potentially dangerous to import systems derived from other needs and out of other circumstances.

For example, a UNESCO publication concerned with counselling and guidance at the higher education level envisaged, for developing countries, a service that would include testing and grading, an information service, counselling and follow-up procedures, research and staff training.[8] Recruits to the training courses would be psychologists or, if not, graduates with one or two years of additional study in psychology. This was seen as taking place 'within the context of life-long learning'. But no mention was made of learning through life. The declared aim was 'that specific educational objectives may be achieved at every stage of the individual's life' with a recommendation that 'guidance programmes should be developed in terms of life-long education which means that such a service must co-operate closely with the work of, on the one hand, . . . agencies who will employ graduates and on the other the secondary schools that "feed" the institutions of higher education'—a conception so narrow as to justify deep apprehension.

Fear of being taken over by a professional interest that would unduly absorb scarce resources is one thing; the need for a genuine counselling service is another and should not be dismissed. The Russell Committee made the point that the limited information service they envisaged 'is not a matter for a clerical assistant but for the professional adult education staff and it should figure appropriately in their training.' The cost of allocating such staff and enhancing its scope might not be as much as might be expected. Clerical staff, receiving nowadays not so much less in terms of salary than the professional educators, are frequently found trying to grapple with enquiries and personal needs, well outside their experience and capacities, to the detriment of the work for which they are primarily engaged. The cost in human terms of an inept service is not quantifiable, but it is patently large.

Counsellors drawn from experienced professional adult education staff, part-time or full-time, would normally have a knowledge of the tutorial needs of their students. Persons selected for training would need to be those who could range in concern beyond the confines of their own subject discipline, more interested to arouse and sustain a learning process than to work wholly within the field of specialist knowledge, ready to learn from students as well as to transmit knowledge to them. Newsome, Thorne and Wyld suggest that the 'counsellor should be a man (sic) of faith . . . in a client's potential for growth,' who knows, 'that change is possible' and who should be 'a forward-moving, socialized, rational being who does not have a fundamental need to hurt either himself or others'.[9] The counsellor 'needs to be warm, approachable, flexible, unafraid of experience and therefore able to incorporate data from his own day-to-day living . . . prepared to enter the counselling situation as a person and not a role-playing professional'—a compound of qualities that practically defines any successful adult education tutor.

Relevant skills

Translated into terms of the specific skills needed by counsellors in adult education and on what they might be based, experience has shown the following aspects to be important.

1 An appreciation of the historical, social and educational backgrounds to people's lives. Some of the social and educational changes that have taken place within the lifetime of adults of different ages have been discussed earlier. A skilled counsellor would probe the layers of such change to establish empathy.

2 Within the scope of adult educational counselling this is more important than an approach through the methods of the psychologist. While not unmindful of ways in which people's varied psychological backgrounds may determine their attitudes and responses in new social and educational situations, it is perhaps more important, as suggested, to learn to see adult students historically. How much the search by women for a new way of life arises from their release from an older identity pattern following on social and technological change has already been considered in Chapter 2. This may be accompanied by psychological problems at times, but they are essentially problems of response to a new environmental situation for a woman and her family. A man, threatened with redundancy in his work, may need help to see this as an opportunity to recast his image of himself and to widen his expectations. He also needs help in developing new skills to do so and to find his way through to a solution that is satisfactory within his circumstances. His redundancy may be economically or technologically determined but he brings to his present difficulties an equipment that was historically determined.

3 Knowledge of the responses of adults to a learning situation, insight into their motives and recognition of the advantages and problems usual in adult learning. With this goes the need to be able to reassure people of the value of their own life-experience in their new approaches to formal learning; that they have been in the habit of absorbing, processing and using new knowledge. Housewives frequently speak of themselves as having become 'cabbages' and need to be reminded that they are managers, teachers, skilled administrators and experts in human relations within their own domestic environments.

4 In approaching a new learning situation confidence ebbs and one feels exposed and vulnerable. The counsellor recognizes this and aims to build up the confidence of enquirers who will usually under-rate, rather than overstate, their capacities, wanting to start where they left off formal learning rather than to take the plunge into new experience.

5 Knowledge of the circumstances of people's lives, the constraints under which they live as workers, family men and women, husbands or wives, with ties across generations, within a community or deliberately apart from one.

6 An appreciation of the cultural diversity within the population and what this implies in the way of educational differences or loss. This need not be a matter of skin colour or a non-English accent. The Russell Report emphasizes, for example, the variability, regionally, of early educational opportunity within our own country. The protective camouflage of uniformity in contemporary dress and appearance may conceal differences of class, nationality, upbringing and life-experience that are vital to the understanding of a person's educational need. The counsellor's antennae are alert for the unexplained cultural difference that could lie behind the enquiry and the unexpressed need.

7 A knowledge of the world of work outside the academic helps the counsellor to get on terms with a person seeking counselling. Educational and vocational needs cannot be separated in this context and enquiries and probings by the counsellor should have some basis in knowledge of the diversities of working life. Over a period of time much can be absorbed from the clientele but the counsellor needs to be receptive of information from a variety of sources, and to be able to apply it.

8 Such a counsellor needs to acquire a wide knowledge of the total educational system and in particular those parts of it that are concerned with after-school education of all kinds. While the collection of data, information brochures and official and other memoranda and their regular updating is important, this must be reinforced by a knowledge of what actually happens in any part of the field. The collection of reference material and the making of contacts with other educational institutions is an important background to the work and money and time needing to be allocated to it.

9 The counsellor needs to have knowledge of employment and training opportunities likely to be open to adults and sources of information about them, including those provided by the Department of Employment and the careers services of local education authorities.

10 Working within the community the counsellor will find it necessary to become familiar with the resources of the community—the social and welfare services and voluntary organizations that cater for a variety of needs and interests.

In acquiring and using these skills a counsellor will develop diagnostic ability in relation to people's particular needs, intellectual resources, difficulties and possible outlets for educational development. But the outcome must be one involving self-diagnosis on the part of each adult as an individual, the counsellor maintaining a positive exploratory relationship throughout, sometimes taking an initiative or making a suggestion, but always concerned not to over-ride or assert a solution. In discussing the extent to which a counsellor can be really free of directing or selecting the thoughts of his client, Trefor Vaughan says:

> Deliberately or inadvertently the counsellor almost certainly does both these things. . . . Counsellors vary greatly in how far they try to do this, or avoid doing so, so it is difficult to say when counselling shades off into a more direct form of guidance.[10]

But he warns later in relation to the problem-centred approach,

> All major problems and decisions . . . that occur in the life of an individual are personal problems and since we may never have enough knowledge about all the facts relevant to major life decisions, their issue involves value-judgments, which all of us must later justify to ourselves and with whose consequences we must live.

Training possibilities

A counsellor will continue to build up knowledge and skill in counselling by following up the subsequent experience and careers of those who have sought guidance. Much of the material of the present study comes from setting up such an evaluation and this with a minimum of resources in money and labour. It is finally our students and those we have tried to help who are our best teachers of counselling. By studying them and their problems and seeking their co-operation we can continue to help them and those who follow them.

To what extent is it possible to provide a suitable training for counsellors in adult education? It is certainly not an impossible task, nor does it demand lengthy specialized training if suitable candidates are selected from the wide variety of talent available within the ranks of tutors and administrators. What is doubtful is whether any course of training developed for other conditions is appropriate in this specialized field. Educational counselling in schools and universities is too related to specific stages of human development and arises within specific institutionalized settings; counselling within a social service provision is concerned with problems that may or may not arise in adult education and are not those for which help is sought primarily from a counsellor in adult education. They may arise, incidentally, but they should not be the basis of training.

The full-time and part-time courses for diplomas in adult education should provide an opportunity. But so far as is known, none of them offers an option in adult education counselling. Merely to incorporate a course of lectures on counselling by an academic specialist in the subject is to open it up to the dangers already discussed. Pragmatic approaches might be better. Students are rarely admitted to diploma courses without experience in the field of adult education. This may be very wide or fairly restricted but all have something to contribute to the exploration of the subject. The setting-up of seminars or symposia in which the needs to be met could be examined and the nature of the services to be provided could be discussed would be a useful beginning. The continuity of a research element in the departments of adult education should provide a means by which the hoped-for resulting development of counselling services could be monitored and progress charted. The Teachers' Centres of local education authorities might also provide points for training and exchange of experience within the confines of limited budgets.

A ray of hope

It is at least encouraging to be able to close this chapter with a welcome, however tardy, contribution from official sources. Speaking to the annual conference of the Association for Adult Education in July 1977, Mr Gordon Oakes, MP, Minister of State in the Department of Education and Science, said:

> Among the Venables Committee's stimulating suggestions was one for a national educational advisory service for adults. Personally I would emphasize action at the local level. The local institute is probably the facet of adult education most commonly known about, most easily found and approached. I suggest that it ought to be possible for the prospective students to find there the basic information he needs about the course he wants—even if the course is available only at another establishment. . . . Information on its own is not enough. There needs also to be an element of counselling at the stage of the first—perhaps timid—enquiry. Adult education staff may need to develop new skills for this work.
>
> Some money would help!

11

In residence - an earlier model

Before considering what has been done and what more might be done to build on the experience of the Fresh Horizons courses it is worth looking at the earlier model offered by the Residential Colleges of Adult Education, of which six were established by voluntary effort at various dates since the beginning of the century. For many years they provided the only opportunities for an intensive, many-faceted renewal of educational experience in fields of arts, humanities and social studies, free from the compulsions of examinations designed as the external attestation of schooling and its immediate continuation.

By the time Fresh Horizons courses were started at the City Lit, the majority of students recruited by the colleges were, in fact, preparing for externally assessed diplomas more or less tailored to their situation and experience. Fircroft College in Birmingham, however, adhered to a one-year course of general education not leading to a particular qualification, and similar opportunities were provided for minority groups elsewhere, particularly at Hillcroft College. It is the more recent experience of these two colleges that is particularly reviewed in this chapter, but a preliminary historical note may help to put it into focus.

In the establishment of the colleges—four in England and one each in Scotland and Wales—it was assumed and formally claimed that common residence was itself an important part of the educational experience, an attitude largely inspired by the dominance, in the educational pecking order of the time, of collegiate life in the older universities. Would-be students were accepted by reference to evidence of educational self-help and commitment to social and community action rather than to performance in academic tests and originally they were not accorded any judgmental certificate or diploma on leaving. Without formal connections, they shared, in the persons of their founders and active supporters, the ethos of one or other of the independent movements promoting non-residential adult education as that term was understood in the first quarter of the twentieth century. Ruskin College, established, in fact, before the turn of the century, had, from the beginning, a more direct connection with working-class politics that has been sustained in close relations with the trade union movement.

In order of their foundation the remaining colleges are: Fircroft (Birmingham); Hillcroft (Surbiton); The Catholic Workers, later Plater College (Oxford); Coleg Harlech (Wales); Newbattle Abbey (Dalkeith, Scotland). Associated with them, although primarily concerned to provide training facilities for the movement that sustained it, was the Co-operative College, established first in Manchester and, after the Second World War, at Stanford Hall, Loughborough. With their declared concentration on 'Workers' education they have long been regarded as a high spot in British adult education and have been progressively more successful in securing support from public funds despite their independent status. In the middle 1960s they were accorded special grants by the Department of Education and Science for the enlargement and improvement of their accommodation, and since 1975 accepted students have qualified automatically for supporting grants from the Department. These grants apart, in 1975–6 the colleges attracted one-sixth of the total money made available for adult education by the central government, although the number of students they accommodated in that year was little more than five hundred.

The circumstances in which a special study was made of Fircroft students in the post-war years are mentioned in the Introduction. In particular, a detailed examination was made of student records in six sample years at five-yearly intervals. It is this material, together with some information culled from recent Hillcroft annual reports, that enables some comparisons to be made with the experience of students on Fresh Horizons courses and particularly with those on the full-time courses started in 1973.

Fircroft—origins and intentions

To sketch its early history in the briefest terms, Fircroft was established by the initiative of George Cadbury and with financial support from him and his associates, in the Selly Oak area of Birmingham, in 1909. Its foundation was influenced by the example of the Danish Folk High Schools as experienced and reported by Tom Bryan, a man of working-class origin with a, then very rare, late-acquired university education and theological training. He was the Warden of the college in the first phase that terminated with the war of 1914–18 and his own death in 1917. In that period there were close links with the National Adult School Union which had been crucial to Bryan's own early development in Leicester and in which the Cadbury family had an established role in the Birmingham area.

The claim of the founders, often repeated in various formulations, was that the college did not come into being to provide an avenue to higher education or vocational upgrading. As late as 1946 this was expressed positively as 'to provide an education in the humanities and in community for men who lack opportunity or inclination for education of a more purely academic kind'. From an early date up to the most recent time, facts have been in conflict with these assumptions, as will appear later.

In the inter-war period the earlier Adult School influence progressively diminished. The ethos of the student body, many of whose members had bitter experience of the prevailing economic depression, was political rather than religious—just under half the students, between 1926 and 1936, were unemployed on entry. But even in the very depth of the depression in 1933, the Warden noted:

> The men who come to Fircroft are very far from being unemployable . . . few will be unemployed when they have left Fircroft a month or two behind them. To some Fircroft will act as a clearing house and quite new opportunities will open before them; some will find what they like and can do well in social work (e.g. in occupational centres); a few, but very few, hardly one a year, may find a road to a university.

There were, in fact, eight former students at universities in 1936, which suggests something more like three a year. Of the more than two hundred men who passed through the college in the decade 1926–36, a third were known to have made pretty radical changes in employment and largely from manual to non-manual occupations with an implied upward shift in socio-economic terms. This perturbed some members of the sponsoring trust and the issue was not dead when the college reopened in 1946 after its war-enforced closure. It is the experience of this third phase in the history of the college between 1946 and 1974 that is most relevant in the present context.

Hillcroft

Hillcroft, originally designated as a college for 'working women', was a later foundation (1920) in which the YWCA played a leading part. The title was formally changed after the Second World War and is now recorded as Hillcroft College (Incorporated). The customary expansion of this is 'A residential college for women's adult education, founded in 1920 and grant-aided by the Department of Education and Science'. After the Second World War it enabled a substantial number of women to qualify themselves for training as mature entrants to teaching. Others later became candidates for an external social studies diploma awarded by London University, requiring a two-year course of study. When the award of this diploma was terminated by the university, the college was able to negotiate a two-year diploma course, validated by the Council for National Academic Awards (CNAA).

Comparisons

In comparing Fresh Horizons students with those from the two residential colleges, some particular facts have to be borne in mind. Fresh Horizons courses, although in the first place dominated by women, are on offer to both sexes equally. Men have, in fact, been more in evidence recently in the grant-aided full-time courses that since 1973 have been most directly comparable to the work of the residential colleges. Fircroft, by custom, but not as a requirement of its constitution, has recruited only men; Hillcroft by definition, only women.

Men on Fresh Horizons courses have characteristically had poorer educational and occupational backgrounds than the women;

limited education and manual work have been preferred recruitment criteria at Fircroft. Hillcroft students are more akin to women Fresh Horizons students than they are to their male residential equivalents at Fircroft as the limited figures in Table 27 indicate.

Table 27 *Comparison of some characteristics of Fircroft and Hillcroft students with those of full-time Fresh Horizons students*

			Fresh Horizons		
		Fircroft	men	women	Hillcroft
	N =	126(a)	22(b)	53(b)	126(c)
		%	%	%	%
ages					
−25		32	9	11	31
25−34		39	45	62	45
35−44		23	41	23	16
45−		6	5	4	8
school-leaving ages					
under 16		66	73	42	34
16 and over		34	27	58	66
post-course studies					
degree level		46	60	74	44(d)
sub-degree level		23	36	9	19

(a) Fircroft students, 1971–2; 1972–3; 1973–4.
(b) Fresh Horizons full-time students, 1973–4; 1974–5, 1975–6.
(c) Hillcroft students, 1974–5; 1975–6.
(d) Hillcroft students completing courses, 1975–6.

Although the grant-aided full-time Fresh Horizons course is a relatively recent development, and the numbers who have taken it are small, it has clearly catered so far for students who, on average, are distinctly older than the students at the two residential colleges. The details are not readily available, but it can be said that this is associated with a higher proportion of young single men and women using the residential courses. They are not proportionately as attractive to older married people.

By the crude test of the proportions of students having minimum schooling or something, not here defined, that is more extensive, there are sex-linked resemblances between students on residential and non-residential courses. Fresh-start courses, whether residential or non-residential, are likely to attract more women than men, with better than minimum schooling, because as a sex, they have a less favourable history of higher education after school-life. So far as post-course entry to formal higher education is evidence of effectiveness, the comparison is favourable to the Fresh Horizons course. It has to be remembered that the Hillcroft figures include twenty-three students who completed two-year CNAA-validated courses in 1976 and that the base for the percentages of them going on to higher education excludes five students who withdrew prematurely during the year. Similar comparisons with Fresh Horizons students attending part-time courses would be less favourable on this score but not markedly so, particularly as regards the evening and more recent day students.

As already indicated, attitudes to academic success at Fircroft, for some of the sponsors at least, have often been ambivalent. Nevertheless, whatever the traditional assumptions—and not all governors and staff members have accepted them—increasing numbers and proportions of Fircroft students, throughout the post-war years, have used their college year as a staging post en route to formal higher education. This has been so although the proportion of students who could unequivocally be described as working men certainly did not decline. In the ten years between 1964–5 and 1973–4, the annual proportion going on to formal higher education rose from one-half to more than two-thirds. Within this changing pattern, there was also a change of emphasis in the direction of more access to degree-level higher education as opposed to non-degree level as Table 28 reveals.

Table 28 *Comparison of Fircroft students (UK entrants) in two three-yearly periods going on to formal higher education*

	1964–5/1966–7	1971–2/1973–4
total students	110	126
going to formal higher education	57 = 51%	87 = 69%
including		
degree level	19 = 17%	58 = 46%
sub-degree level	38 = 34%	29 = 23%

One of the allegations of the tutors and students, whose disruptive activities in 1975 resulted in temporary closure of the college, was that students were being pressured into seeking academic higher education and that, in the process, they were detaching themselves from their working-class origins. Thereby, it was alleged, the declared intentions of the college sponsors were being denied. Ironically these complaints coincided with strong efforts by the Principal to increase recruitment of older, trade union activists, who were most likely, by reason of age, family commitments and occupational backgrounds, to return to their original or similar occupations on completion of their studies. The detailed examination of student histories in six sample years at five-year intervals in the post-war period produced a pattern of probabilities as to leaving intentions that can be summarized as follows, although the word 'probabilities' must be strongly emphasized:

More likely to:	*Personal characteristics*			
	age-group	marital status	occupation	schooling
return to old or new work	older	married	manual	minimum
proceed to further education/training *below* degree-level		no marked distinctions		
proceed to degree-level further education	younger	single	non-manual	above minimum

Deliberate recruitment by reference to social and occupational origins and background clearly differentiated practice at Fircroft from that of the promoters of Fresh Horizons courses. In view of the relatively small number of men recruited by the latter it might be argued that most men seeking anything like the same educational experience prefer the company of their own sex, and, as indicated in Chapter 9, there is evidence that some men, at least, found it difficult to acclimatize themselves to the company of more capable or educationally better-prepared women. Moreover, the male equivalents of many of the women presenting themselves for the Fresh Horizons courses, would, almost certainly, have benefited from the extended access to direct continuative higher education more widely available to their sex. Fircroft recruitment, almost by definition, included a higher proportion of students with basic deficiencies of earlier education likely to need the more extended and intensive renewal of education that a full-time residential course should apparently permit. It would seem, also, that the mutual aid that adult students extend to one another, as the Fresh Horizons students testify, could be enhanced in such a situation.

These are relevant considerations, but some caveats must be entered. Fircroft is not unique in finding that the older pattern of residence by the term, with a plethora of non-curricular communal activities, has largely given way to residence by the week, as a matter of convenience rather than of educational principle. At Fircroft, the increase in more recent years of the number of men with family commitments, coupled with the ubiquity of private car ownership and a motor-way network, effectively reduced the pro-grammed working week to four-and-a-half days.

Even more decisively, the Hillcroft annual report for 1975–6 notes that of sixty-six students who completed the year, 'thirty-nine were resident: twenty-seven attended daily'. Of five who with-drew prematurely during the year, four were resident. Continuous residence, increasingly rejected by university students, simply does not fit with the common pattern of women's lives as it has deve-loped over recent years.

Unlike Fircroft, Hillcroft, as already indicated, provides two-year CNAA-validated courses offering diplomas, side-by-side with a traditional one-year non-diploma course. Only eight of the sixty-six students who completed the 1975–6 year were on the one-year course. Of the thirty-six women who enrolled in that year for the first year of a diploma course, eleven withdrew, two of them during and nine at the end of the year, leaving twenty-five to go forward to the second year.

The limitations that such changes are placing on traditional assumptions about the educational advantages of residence inevit-ably bring in question its inescapably escalating cost and enforce comparisons with the costs of non-residential equivalents. In Table 29 the Fircroft and Hillcroft figures are derived from pub-lished accounts. The Fresh Horizons figures are based on ascertained costs of salaries and associated charges for full- and part-time staff and on official estimates of student-hour unit costs for other elements of expenditure. The allocation of tuition costs to 'Grant-aided FT (full-time) students only', probably errs on the high side.

Table 29 *Comparison of expenditure and costs per student, Fircroft College and City Lit Fresh Horizons courses, 1973–4 and Hillcroft College, 1975–6*

	gross costs			costs per student			
	tuition	other	total	tuition	other	total	net*
	£	£	£	£	£	£	£
Fresh Horizons (full-time equiv. all students— 40.75)	7,100	2,520	9,620	174	62	236	236
(grant-aided full-time students—25)	5,150	1,545	6,695	206	62	268	268
Fircroft (full-time equiv. students—47)	23,400	46,100	69,500	498	981	1,479	1,303
Hillcroft (†) (full-time equiv. students—68.3)	46,500	56,000	102,500	680	820	1,500	1,317

* Net amount per student chargeable to public funds (excluding personal and family maintenance grants).

† Hillcroft students numbers include proportionate allowances for those withdrawing prematurely.

Hillcroft tuition costs must include a considerable element of additional inflation between 1974 and 1976.

Such bare comparisons leave plenty of room for argument as to whether like is being compared with like but, with a difference in public cost ratio in the order of five to one, the differential advantages of residential over non-residential provision need to be very large and clearly evident when any further allocation of public money for adult education is in prospect.

And all the more so since students at residential colleges now qualify for mandatory grants whether actually 'resident' or not. It is hard to see why full-time Fresh Horizons students should remain dependent, as they now are, on the increasingly uncertain discretion of local education authorities. Students on part-time Fresh Horizons courses are of course at the other extreme. It is taken for granted that they will both meet their own expenses and pay a course fee. At the City Lit this has been minimal, but the national picture is one of reduced budgets and largely increased fees and both are calculated to militate against the establishment of more fresh start courses.

It has also to be remembered that in the full period of the Fresh Horizons year, something like one hundred students are receiving tuition, tutoring and counselling. Additionally the tutors' expertise is available to a 'drop-in' of enquirers and to those who make use of the general counselling service that is on offer from the Fresh Horizons staff. It can certainly be argued that the staffing has been inadequate, being based too rigidly on a formula taken from another educational context and housed, as it has been, within the Cinderella section of non-vocational education—generous though London's is compared with the country at large. There would be plenty of leeway for improvement without approaching the residential level of tuition cost per student.

When the members of the Russell Committee accepted the need for limited residential provision 'to safeguard the special needs' of 'a minority group',[1] they were properly impressed by past achievement, but singularly unaware of its contemporary inadequacy. To be generous to a few hundred 'late developers' implies no great criticism of the early education that failed them; to admit failure on a scale that the response to Fresh Horizons and similar courses already makes apparent is quite another matter, and quite outside the ability of residential colleges to remedy. But pending a far more widespread provision of appropriate non-residential courses some fortunate individuals have reason to be thankful for what there is.

12

Alternative routes

This study is based directly on one contemporary example of what is commonly discussed as 'second-chance' education. It has also looked briefly at an older version in different settings and at some wider issues that are particularly illustrated by these examples.

It remains to consider what has hitherto contributed to restricting educational provision of such clearly demonstrated value and the indications there are of new trends and wider possibilities that should be encouraged.

Second chance—a misnomer

It is unfortunate that the Russell Committee gave renewed currency to the term 'second chance', merely demurring, in the interests of its concern for the concept of *education permanente*, that the 'term is not to be interpreted strictly: the need may equally be for third, fourth or n^{th} chances'.[1] Philip Hopkins, then principal, writing in his Fircroft College report for 1964–5, objected to the term for other reasons. 'First', he writes, 'there is a flavour of patronage—you missed your first chance by failing eleven plus or early school-leaving; now is your chance to redeem yourself.' For many Fircroft students, he contends, a 'first chance' was never really presented. 'How or where', he asks, 'did Jim Ingram miss his first chance?[2] By being born a cripple, or by selecting estranged parents or by going nearly blind through cataracts when in his teens?' He also notes that, 'the ideas roused by the phrase . . . are not normally those associated with enrichment of the personality but rather with material enrichment.' It implies, 'that those students who do not make (immediate) vocational use of their residential studies have missed their chance and wasted not only their time but considerable public money.'

The phrase is, indeed, curiously equivocal with implications of free-will that have adhered to the word 'chance' throughout the vagaries of English usage. It is perhaps most commonly thought of as meaning opportunity, something that you may or may not take but which has its end in something good. To have ignored your first chance is to have wasted an opportunity. To have a second chance carries with it an uncomfortable sense of the schoolmaster's 'your last chance'. As Hopkins says, 'there is an air of finality about the phrase.' But the primary meaning of the word 'chance' is not an opportunity-to-be-taken but a 'fortuitous circumstance', 'an undesigned happening'—in derivation, 'the way the dice fell', bound up with uncertainty and containing no element of free-will as in the Book of Common Prayer's, 'the changes and chances of this mortal life' and often implying something less than beneficial. Used in this sense the term could imply not only the hazards of early educational experience but also the rare likelihood of meeting with renewed opportunities of the right kind in adult life.

It is, as Hopkins says, patronizing, and attaches to itself patronizing overtones as when the Russell Committee advocates residential college provision for 'the adult who, for whatever reason, did not take the normal route onwards from school'.[3] Was the Russell Committee nodding so hard at this point that it forgot that 'the normal route onwards from school' for over two-thirds of school-leavers, even in 1973, was straight out into the working world; that less than one-third went into any form of full-time further education and that 70 per cent of children in that year left school at age 16 or under? The report continues, 'It is essential to keep an alternative route for adult late developers, especially those from unpropitious environments whose perceptions of the possibility of higher education come only in mature life.' These echoes of nineteenth-century phraseology are all the more odd because they contrast with the account of educational deprivation or inadequacy, surviving into adult life, well-presented elsewhere in the report and already quoted in Chapter 2. Indeed the report makes the further point, that:

The concept of education continuing throughout life must include a conscious missionary effort towards all who were lost at the earlier stages and there will be a persisting need for remedial adult education of imaginative and varied kinds. This will apply with particular emphasis to disadvantaged and handicapped groups and also to those who happened to be born too early to benefit from educational reform. For it has to be remembered that such reforms take more than a generation to work through the population. In the meantime their effect is frequently not towards the unifying of society but towards the accentuation of differences. The enlargement of opportunity for some may mean the reinforcement of disadvantage for others and the consequent sharpening of the need for remedial provision. The Swedish concept, of an adult's entitlement to the equivalent of the basic minimum of education, rising as that minimum is raised for the children, has much to commend it.[4]

To take only one example: the doubling of the number of girls having 'A' level passes on leaving school in 1973 in comparison with those leaving ten years earlier and the 50 per cent increase in the number of boys similarly qualified, should surely have alerted university authorities and others to the existence and needs of a reserve of potential students no less capable intellectually than those coming straight from the school gates. But, in fact, those who left earlier without the sacred symbols, have, to all intents and purposes, been written off. If they have the temerity to challenge, they are too commonly met only with insensitive discouragement.

The Russell Committee asked for:

An integrated education system (that) will involve postponing to adult stages of life certain educational experiences that are appropriate to the needs of maturity. Included among these will be second and third chances for those whose first choice has led to a dead end; opportunities for updating in the many fields where knowledge is continually developing; opportunities for trying out one's ability to study in a new field before committing oneself to it; activities related to specifically adult responsibilities like parenthood and citizenship; and studies involving value judgments that require maturity of experience for their comprehension. The need here, in terms of the educational system, is for a planned quaternary stage of education, identifiably *adult*.[5]

The GCE route march

Given this liberality of language, it is strange that, in summing up how needs are to be met, the concept of second chance education is confined to 'the opportunity to acquire qualifications whose relevance to the individual has become clear in adult life'[6] and that nowhere is the total need adequately explored. But, even though restricted by its terms of reference to the strait-jacket of 'non-vocational' adult education, the committee was inescapably compelled to glance at the shifts made by adults to fulfil the entry requirements for higher education and training, the standards of which have risen steadily over the years. The report points out that university extra-mural departments and the residential colleges have, in fact, despite their non-vocational slotting, created and prepared students for certificates and diplomas as end-products to their courses[7]—hence the various diploma courses at all, save one, of the residential colleges and the social work and youth-leaders' courses leading to qualifications of many of the extra-mural departments. Nevertheless, because of attempted purist distinctions between vocational and non-vocational education, adults seeking entry tickets to higher education have needed to resort, in the main, to colleges of further education, whose primary concern has been with 16–19-year-olds on full- or part-time GCE and lower-level vocational courses.

Although adults have frequently made special niches for themselves in such colleges, the courses devised for them have conformed to the designs established for use in schools and in schools, moreover, where streaming has predestined children of certain ages, abilities and aptitudes to seek certain defined goals. Some colleges, for example, will specify a two-year course for 'A' levels because it is a two-year programme in schools, where it is set in a context that includes games, optional studies, participation in school clubs and the social training of the young. A full-time course of 'O' level subjects often restricts adults to the limits of what is demanded from 16-year-olds at the end of four or five years of secondary schooling. With the establishment since 1965 of the

CSE as an alternative school-leaving qualification, some colleges of further education are now even offering a late students' access to that. Within the school assessment system, arbitrary decisions have, inevitably, to be made as to whether a student is entered for the higher or the lower rating qualification. How much more difficult is it for such decisions to be made by or on behalf of the mixed bag of adults who appear on enrolment nights to join classes in colleges of further education? The experience of the Fresh Horizons and residential college courses is that the apparent level of achievement at the end of school life is no predictor of mature academic potential. Nor is the immediate response to the course: some, particularly those with lesser academic skills to call on, take time to reveal their capacity, but they need themes to work on big enough to challenge them into reading, thinking and writing at a mature level and to acquire the skills they lack, in doing so. Time, too, is of the essence for mature students: having already given ten, fifteen, twenty or more years to productive work for society it is a poor reward to be sent back to the school curriculum as the only way to develop under-used capacities.

Yet it has to be recognized that, for various reasons, mature people have sought endorsement of their abilities by certification. With 80 per cent of school-leavers now claiming some paper qualification, however limited its significance must be for many of them, there is pressure on the non-certificated adults to maintain their self-respect by producing evidence, satisfying to themselves and others, of their ability to meet this younger generation on terms of equality in work and society. The statistics published by the Department of Education and Science give no information about the number of adults who offer themselves as candidates for GCE examinations at 'O' and 'A' levels, although the facts must be known to the various examining boards. Yet it is known that quite large numbers do so to gain required qualifications for professional registration, to set a seal on a late-acquired proficiency in a skill or a language or simply to satisfy themselves that they are educable in modern terms as they apply to their children. For many people it has been a useful ladder and, for many purposes, the only acknowledged means of renewal education. Adults who may possess school-leaving qualifications, now overtaken by later innovations deemed to be of a higher status, also wish to reassure themselves or to justify their ability to enter professional training or higher education. Merely to list a variety of adult courses taken over the years, does not provide that reassurance to themselves or to others. 'I've been to a lot of classes but have nothing to show for it', was one student's express complaint. That she had actually enjoyed them was, in a way, a further diminution of their value, enjoyment in education being somewhat suspect.

Adapting the system

The Russell Committee welcomed, 'experiments being made by certain of the examining boards in devising [GCE] courses of a more flexible character and forms of assessment appropriate to adults'[8] and recommended these to colleges of further education. A number of experiments have been made to fill the gap in this way. These have included linked radio and correspondence courses that can lead to specially devised 'O' levels in home and community education and decision-making and broadcast foreign language programmes for which an examinations board has offered optional testing, though not related to 'O' level qualification.

Multi-media courses of the kinds mentioned take much preparation time and demand a concentration of diverse skills to mount successfully. Moreover, broadcasting time for such ventures is limited and there are many interests competing for it. They can, however, reach students not reached, or reachable in other ways. They can also provide a tangible end-product for the student who wants something to show for her involvement in liberal studies.

Examining bodies have also devised alternative English syllabuses for mature students and extensions of this principle are proposed by the Joint Matriculation Board for subjects such as archaeology and psychology which are known to attract adults to non-examination classes.

There are several dangers adhering to such an approach. Examination-bound syllabuses, however liberal in scope, can become an inhibiting element within an adult study group which by the nature of its membership, diverse in experience and voluntary in attendance, is exploratory in its learning. Furthermore, an examining body, in seeking to achieve content and examining standards outside its known area of formal schooling, may lean over backward to be academically acceptable. It may therefore devise syllabuses and expect responses that go beyond those normally expected of 'O' level candidates: it may indeed get such responses. Many students may be examined at a lower level than their developing capacities warrant and receive a reward incommensurate with them. It has been observed how at adult residential colleges and within the Fresh Horizons courses some students with little formal early education will achieve first-year university level within a year of full-time or part-time study. There is, further, an organizational element to consider. Even with the aid of broadcasting and special texts, new 'O' level courses have to overcome the inertia of established teaching and administrative arrangements. They may be accepted as part of a college syllabus, but it is doubtful whether the scale of offering could be such as would provide for the situations in which people are required to produce substantial evidence of capacity to undertake higher education or professional training, especially if time is limited. For the adult student in a hurry, a concentration on correspondence, or college, mainstream GCE courses would still be the answer. It might not be as educationally satisfying, but that is one of the hazards of imposing entry tickets at any age.

It is possible, in fact, that if basic factual material has to be assimilated as a necessary preliminary to satisfy a career choice already made, the normal GCE route may be the least cumbersome way for the mature student. It is not the best route and professional and other bodies should look closely at what they are demanding from mature applicants. And all the more so since entry requirements tend to rise with the rising supply of young people with higher school-leaving qualifications, who are not necessarily thereby any more able than their forerunners. Adults with limited prewar schooling, attending Fresh Horizons courses, frequently found that, with a minimum of self-directed preparation, they could enter privately for 'O' and sometimes 'A' level examinations and pass well enough to establish new confidence in themselves.

The Venables Report

The Open University's Committee on Continuing Education has had these questions under consideration. Its interim report says, of the kind of qualifications typified by the GCE examinations and their equivalents, that:

> they are designed as terminal qualifications for school-
> children and, while many adults may attempt them (for want

of any alternative) they are, in consequence, frequently unsuitable for adults. Courses can be designed, at various levels of intellectual challenge, specifically for adults, dealing with subjects of adult concern and assessed by methods related to adult needs.[9]

The report continues:

> The Committee considers that the provision of [such] courses
> . . . is a development that the Open University should amplify on sound academic grounds, which could provide the basis for assessment at nationally recognized level. Such courses should have a high priority in taking into account the growing desire in the adult education field to respond to the needs of learners, as expressed by themselves, rather than to make a provision of prescriptive courses which leave no room for individual development and exploration.[10]

In its subsequent report, however, the Committee recommends that 'the Open University should pursue exploratory schemes of collaboration with a number of examination boards and should lend strong support to any moves made nationally to provide accreditation of adult-conceived courses at standards equivalent to GCE "O" and "A" grades'[11]—a far from open concept.

Historically, the adult residential colleges have provided the most obvious chance for academically unqualified adults seeking opportunities of returning to sustained learning. Their long record and the debts that some legislators and leaders in public life owe to them has tended almost to adulation of this form of provision. Yet the Russell Committee was not greatly enamoured of its extension, recommending only one more college to provide for a better geographical spread, which might bring the total of available places in England, Wales and Scotland to something like six hundred. Doubts about this kind of provision have been explored in Chapter 11. The logical answer to increased need, the unsuitability of school-related examinations and a larger potential demand should, in terms of modern living, be the encouragement and financing of non-residential opportunities of a similar kind.

Initiatives

The Russell Committee's blinkered vision when looking at what it calls 'second chance' education is all the more difficult to understand in that, while it was sitting, the Open University was already admitting its first academically untested students to full university courses. Indeed the Committee did make a tentative mention of the effect of the Open University in creating a demand for preliminary courses, noting that their provision had been stimulated in many centres and that:

> there is an increasing range of other courses of preliminary study including an impressive development of day-time courses for women who wish to be teachers or social workers. There is also evidence that, where facilities of this kind are provided with a view to qualifications, they draw an appreciable number of 'eavesdropping' students whose interest is solely in the study itself and not in the qualification.[12]

No discussion follows of the need to satisfy more than an eaves-dropping interest nor is there any recognition that the development of such courses might be a new starting point in adult education.

Those who have followed the GCE route have followed an obvious and accessible way rather than specified a demand for a preferable alternative. Even a fairly knowledgeable member of the general public, however, would find it difficult to articulate a need for return to education on a broad base that enabled advances to be made without reference to an educational starting point and a qualifying finishing post. But there is good evidence that, if the providers publicize an offer in such terms as 'Fresh Start', 'New Opportunities for Adults' or 'Returning to Learning', a lot of people will recognize it as addressed to them.

Such courses have appeared and are continuing to appear from a variety of institutions offered on terms that reflect the nature and resources of the providing source. Adult education centres, extra-mural departments of universities, colleges of education (as part of their new output) and at least one polytechnic are among them. Courses are usually confined to part-time study on one, two or three shortened days or lengthened evenings, and hours of attendance are chosen with domestic responsibilities in mind. Some are as short as five weeks, but a period of at least two terms of twelve weeks would seem to be almost the minimum required to develop a real learning experience of some depth. A week's full-time residential summer school can be a useful testing ground.

Course components

With stress laid variously on different aspects, the following course components can be distinguished:

1 A core of compulsory subjects, studied at an adult level with a group of tutors working as a team, the aim being to stretch the mind, broaden the understanding and develop reading and communication skills, including those of numeracy that will provide the tools for further learning.

2 Initial counselling interviews with prospective students of whom no previous academic qualifications are asked but from whom basic literacy is required.

3 The establishment of an unstreamed, participatory group of students committed to regular attendance at classes and to serious reading and written work at home.

4 The close monitoring by tutors of the work of students whose needs for individual tutorial help, counselling and career advice are provided for during the course.

5 Willingness to act as referee for students during and after the course, providing an assessment of their capacities and personal qualities to accompany applications for training, jobs or higher education. One of the many obstacles to starting again is the lack of recent or appropriate referees.

6 Recognition that the process is a developmental one that can continue in a variety of ways when the course comes to an end, this starting of a process and not the acquisition of a college diploma or public examination success, to be the emphasized intention of the course.

Some examples

When a Fresh Start course was established at the Richmond Adult College in 1976, these features were clearly indicated to prospective students. They were adopted, not without initial hesitations, by a group of tutors whose previous experience had been closely geared to the teaching of specialist subjects for GCE examinations or to extra-mural university or college non-examination classes. The criteria for the new venture were expressed in the following way:

> Though the course is a part-time one it must provide for a very substantial commitment in time and effort by the

students. The aim is to achieve in one session of two terms, an immersion in study equivalent to several years of part-time study of GCE subjects taken *seriatim*. Some students will make a break-through to first-year university level and others will be well on the way to it. For them and the others on the course, a raised level of understanding should be achieved that will continue to serve as a critical standard for future learning and interpretation of life experience.

To enable students to have a knowledge of choice and some capacity to tackle advanced study in one of a number of academic fields, the course needs to consist of a group of subjects, all of which must be taken. Each subject should be studied in depth rather than covered superficially over a wide syllabus.

In each part of the course, the promotion of literacy and oracy at a discriminating level and, as appropriate, numeracy, should be implicit.

Tutorial staff, all of whom will bear a responsibility for the personal help and guidance that students will be encouraged to seek must bear in mind that students will be of varying abilities and educational experience.

Emphasis on interaction between tutors and students in a learning situation rather than on formal teaching should provide continuous feed-back on the progress of students and on the course as a whole.

Team teaching and tutorial supervision are implicit in the concept of the course and provision must be made for staff meetings and consultations within normal teaching hours. A co-ordinating tutor must have the responsibility for seeing that these take place.

Students will need to discuss their post-course objectives: the co-ordinating tutor in consultation with other members of the staff will demonstrate an interest in students that will help them to sort out their aims and so provide a continuous counselling service of information and advice in relation to them.

What finally evolved, in this instance, out of the teaching, physical and financial resources of the college was a one-day-a-week (Tuesdays) course from 10 a.m. to 3.15 p.m., lasting 30 weeks and based on English (language and literature combined) and social and economic studies and psychology, in which mathematics as a practical tool of learning was introduced, together with techniques of library use, counselling and career advice. A further day or evening attendance at an optional class was an integral part of the course. This was chosen with the help of the course tutor, from the college's total offering of foreign languages, skills and crafts, GCE studies and liberal arts classes.

The Nelson and Colne College in Lancashire has a rather different approach. A tertiary college, providing full-time and part-time education for all post-16-year-old students in its catchment area, it aims, in the terms of its prospectus, to meet, 'the educational, social and recreational needs of the community through further education'. It shows a special concern for adult returners in its Open College provision, a rolling programme of two-stage courses, that, completed satisfactorily, is accepted as an adult equivalent of 'A' levels as an entry qualification for degree courses at co-operating institutions. It is notable that, in this complex enterprise, with a heavy loading of 16- to 19-year-olds in part-time and full-time courses, including pre-university study of GCE subjects, adults have been accorded separate provision and have not been expected to follow the conventional route set for their juniors.

A course, related in intent but differing in scope has been mounted at Hatfield Polytechnic since 1971.[13] Students attend the 'New Opportunities for Women' (NOW) course from 10 a.m. to 3 p.m., one day a week for ten weeks. The day is divided into four sessions of one hour. In the first hour students have a series of lectures on relevant aspects of industrial and occupational psychology leading to a survey of women's employment. In the second and third hours, two guest speakers talk to the students about the career and training opportunities in their fields. In the last hour students form three groups and, together with a tutor, discuss anything they choose or prepare seminar papers on selected topics. Aptitude and interest tests can be taken, administered by the qualified polytechnic staff, whose counsellors are also available for consultation.

The NOW course gave birth to 'Polyprop', described as a preparatory course for mature students contemplating enrolment at the Hatfield Polytechnic's degree and diploma courses, offering, on two shortened days a week for five weeks, a lightning introduction to study for those who, one supposes, must already have a fairly clear picture of what they want to do and be capable to some extent of tackling it, though this course, too, will no doubt attract its eavesdroppers.

Avery Hill College of Education, at its annexe in the East End of London has, since the Autumn of 1976, offered what it calls a 'Second Chance' course of six terms, each of ten weeks. Required studies are fitted into two half-days or two evenings a week over two years. They extend to English language, sociology, mathematics, and what in the prospectus is described as 'Patterns of thought in the twentieth century'. An additional optional subject has to be chosen from a wide offering that includes art, languages and science. There are no entry or exit qualifications but students are promised a detailed assessment at the end of the course, which is described as being, 'of value to future employers or for possible admission to polytechnics or universities as an alternative to formal examination qualifications'.

A university extra-mural variant comes from the University of Newcastle-upon-Tyne Department of Adult Education.[14] Since 1974 the department has offered 'New Opportunities' courses of one day a week for twenty weeks, each day consisting of three one-and-a-half hour periods. Two of these are devoted to academic studies which involve students in systematic reading, discussion and writing based on literature and politics. The third period of each day is used for advice on areas of employment, voluntary activity and further education and training. Time is made—with difficulty—in this period for individual counselling. Reporting on the first seven courses, the tutors make an observation that confirms what has already been indicated and that needs to be continuously borne in mind when such courses are in contemplation: 'What has become increasingly clear is that measures of previous educational attainment give an imperfect guide to the level at which students operate. Other factors are work experience, voluntary and community involvement and marriage'—to which could well be added, family commitments and child rearing.

Many preparatory courses are now available in adult centres for Open University applicants. The Open University Committee's *Interim Report on Continuing Education*[15] quotes a figure of 4,000 students on preparatory and introductory courses at local centres in 1975. Usually mounted in the Autumn term in anticipation of the Open University's academic year beginning in February, and consisting of twelve class meetings, they attract a wider range of students than the successful applicants for Open University undergraduate courses for whom they are primarily intended. Limited in time, they are concerned, in the main, with techniques of study, content serving as illustrative material to that end. A Return to Study course of two evening hours over a period of ten weeks at the Department of Adult Education at the University of Leicester has followed this pattern.

The Committee on Continuing Education also cites 3,000 students studying by means of National Extension College (NEC) correspondence courses that are described as suitable preparation for enrolment with the Open University. The NEC, a non-profit-making institution, has also promoted Saturday Schools and face-to-face tutorial aid for its students, at colleges of further education and adult institutes. Additionally it runs its own weekend residential schools to provide personal contact with tutors and the group dynamism so often missing from lone students' lives. The 'Returning to Learning' intensive week's summer school, held annually at the Loughborough University of Technology since 1971, deploys a variety of learning tools—film, tape, reading, essay-writing, lectures, group discussion, library use, and underpins the course with personal tutorials and counselling.

In addition to the break into full-time non-residential courses represented by the City Lit Fresh Horizons course, Paddington College in London has started a full-time 'Careers Foundation Course' on similar lines. Full maintenance grants are available to students on both these courses but, as yet, only on a disadvantageous discretionary basis compared with the mandatory grants now available to students of the residential colleges.[16] In Northern Ireland, Magee College, Londonderry, under the wing of the University of Ulster, provides a two-year part-time and a one-year full-time course for a Certificate of Continuing Education.

Administrative schizophrenia

These ventures, all of which aim to promote continuing or recurrent education as an end in itself but which increasingly act as launching pads for adults into higher education and training, do not derive from any national statement of policy. The Russell

Committee was too bound up with existing forms of provision, and its dominant and surviving members too representative of them, to point strongly in new directions. The setting-up of the Open University was a unique governmental adventure into the outer space of education and in outcome very far removed from the concept originally mooted by Sir Harold Wilson. It has been the personal imagination of ordinary working part-time and full-time staffs in the field that has cozened new enterprises out of resources that have always been threatened and have always needed to be thinly spread.

Apart from the Open University, and at the other end of the scale the adult literacy campaign, government initiative has been concentrated on the reorganization of the manpower services and the provision of vocational training schemes to meet specific shortages in a worsening employment situation. These can, however, promote basic educational skills for those whose employment is jeopardized by their lack. The Training Opportunities Scheme (TOPS) can provide a mild shot-in-the-arm for further and adult education institutions mounting training and pre-TOPS courses, but the attitude is basically utilitarian and there is no certainty of continuing support for an institution's work as a whole. Similarly the money allocated for a limited term for the support of the adult literacy campaign provided nothing for general administration of the operative institutions.

The division of administrative responsibility for vocational education and training between the Departments of Employment and of Education and the making of special grants for specific purposes also create new complexities. Distinctions are made between students, some receiving not only free education or training but maintenance and travel grants during the course, while others pay yearly-increasing fees to establish their learning skills as a prelude to improving their employment possibilities. Similarly there are distinctions between full-time and part-time students determining the help they can obtain in favour of the former, when part-time study is often the necessary starting point for women making a phased return to life and work outside the home. There are distinctions between courses in institutions with the balance of staff and use of other resources being tipped by financial considerations and there are educationally untenable distinctions between providing bodies and institutions. Such discrimination derives from the powers possessed and the way they are used by the Education and Employment Ministries respectively. But within the educational service itself administrative distinctions create constraints that at present contribute to forming the mould into which continuing education is forced. The status of colleges of further education, and the remuneration of the staff they employ, are directly related to the standard and volume of work they conduct, assessed in terms of recognized examinations. Unit totals based on student hours are enhanced by full-time courses that can be related to higher-level study within the examination system. This acts as a deterrent to the setting-up of part-time courses, the difficult work with those of low academic skills and the promotion of uncertificated adult education.

This discrimination continues in the charges made to students who are frequently required to pay less for a so-called 'vocational' GCE course (even if they are purely eavesdroppers) than they do for a non-examination class, tailored to adult needs, that may be more demanding of effort by students and tutors. Furthermore, when economies are imposed on further education, they are always made disproportionately on the non-examination adult side of the work. But for these crippling distinctions there would be much more incentive for enterprising adult departments of colleges of further education to promote courses of the Fresh Horizons type.

Open college concepts

The unquestioned success of the Open University, within the limits assigned to it, has encouraged the idea that there might be a development on parallel lines operating at different or, in educational hierarchical terms, lower levels—the 'analogues' of the Russell Report.[17] This is one of the concepts that has given rise to the use of the words 'Open College' to designate a restatement of adult education that would provide for mature educational needs at sub-university levels. Some have seen this not so much as a restatement but as a newly devised access to education based essentially on the broadcasting services and correspondence and exploiting all forms of educational technology.

There is undeniable force in the conception of an Open College as a distinct and separate development much as the Open University necessarily was if it was to escape from the diffused motive power of existing institutions and generate its own head of steam. But any concept of an Open College has to take into account a much wider range of functions to be performed for a differently motivated clientele. Unlike the Open University offering its clients a defined objective, primarily a first degree, an Open College would need to be wide open in scope, multi-level, multi-purpose and unstratified. Open University students are highly motivated and, as Naomi McIntosh has pointed out, they are also unusual people:

> Open University students are not only not typical of conventional university students but are also not typical of their contemporaries in the community at large. From whatever background they come, they have already displayed a propensity to learn which is remarkable.[18]

The Open University model, in short, is based on a highly motivated, dedicated and self-disciplining body of students, fairly certain of their intention and able to pursue individual studies with a minimum of direction.

It is much less certain that Open College students would or should be processed in the same way. The Open College should not be defined in terms implying merely a convenient mode of preparation for the Open University, nor yet as 'Son of Open University', using similar techniques and co-existing on distant but privileged terms with the traditional providers of further and adult education and the Open University itself.

The open network

As an alternative, some people have seen and presented the Open College as a convenient hold-all for the variety of desirable educational experience over the whole of a working life and the provision to be made for it. Emphasis would be on provision meeting immediate practical needs and yet capable of being integrated into a developmental system; it would be nation-wide and even international in acceptance but local in its direction; capable of using distance teaching but linked to community institutions. Implicit in such a concept is the restructuring of relationships on a basis of equality between all the elements in the existing network of post-school education whether labelled vocational, non-vocational, further, technical or adult and the nurturing of new developments

stemming from experiments made possible by co-operation between them. They would form a network held together by a common information centre or centres and with linked counselling
arrangements. This is a concept that challenges everyone concerned with post-compulsory education to examine demands,
assess priorities and work out a strategy for promoting common
purposes in relation to them. It was, after all, such considerations
that induced the Russell Committee to give high priority to the
concept of a National Development Council for Adult Education.

Legitimate concern for the post-school education of the 16- to
19-year-olds should not be allowed to cloud the issue. Their
problems derive, in part, from tasks the schools left unfinished, the
imperfect acquisition of basic skills and uncompleted socialization.
It is the job of the colleges of further education, employers, training boards and the Department of Employment, or other like
bodies, to meet the educational and training needs of young people
not yet bearing the responsibilities of adult life although often
claiming its privileges. The needs of adults voluntarily seeking
continued development throughout life in all its aspects, vocational, personal and social, are of a different kind. They arise in
part out of the opportunity gap between generations but, above all,
they arise out of living itself. Desire for knowledge is whetted by
experiences of work and leisure, by the intensities of family life and
the changing shape and demands of society. Men and women need
to be encouraged to believe that such desires are wholesome and
legitimate and to be given tools of education proper to their needs.

Under-used capacity

In relation to both national needs and to personal fulfilment, in
modern terms, we are an under-educated people. But in regard to
women we are not prepared to use even the minimum education
with which we have equipped them and acknowledge as their due.
They comprise half at least of the national intelligence and the
gross failure to use them in positions of responsibility puts a
heavier burden on the men who, with no more aggregate intellectual power, must be relied on to take the ultimate decisions that
determine every aspect of our communal life.

It is no longer a valid excuse to say that in rearing the next
generation, women are adequately discharging their responsibili-

ties. Increasingly, this is now a function that occupies only a decade of women's lives: the most recent demographic trends show that fertility control and conscious family planning are now the norms in all social groups.[19] The situation is one of evolutionary significance: educationally it is not merely inadequate so much as positively dangerous to make placatory gestures to unfilled leisure—to offer them 'courses of evening instruction specially designed to render liberal instruction agreeable', in James Joyce's mordant phrase.[20]

For men it is perhaps a less inappropriate prescription. The incidence of unemployment falls unevenly and there is serious conjecture about the continuing capacity of society to set men to productive work as a full life-occupying role. Up to now, adult education for men has been overwhelmingly concerned with employment. There may still be a need for this and indeed for an expansion of that part of it that is directed towards management skills and deeper understanding of human relations. But the idea of paid educational leave should certainly not be seen only in terms of more specific vocational training. It could also be the occasion, as under- and unemployment may provide continuing opportunity, for the deeper consideration of aspects of social change. For example, men have seized hold of the greater sexual freedom of the permissive society, but need to learn to accept concomitant responsibilities to replace those imposed willy-nilly on the traditional breadwinner and family man. Perhaps they need to be released from their breadwinning, as women are in process of being released from domestic toil and child-bearing, so that they can have opportunities to develop skill and pleasure in the crafts, arts and liberal studies interests that, in recent years, have been so largely the preserve of women in adult education centres. Too often men have had to wait for retirement to adventure much in these ways and some levelling up of opportunities between the sexes seems to be called for.

These are by no means Utopian ideas, nor are we devoid of facilities and resources for their exploitation. We may well be dubious about concentrating exclusively on job creation and manpower redeployment in skills for which the need may be disappearing as men and women emerge from the training centres. As to resources, if we care to deploy them, we are faced rather with an embarrassing surplus than with a deficiency. The expansion of the tertiary range of education in the late 1960s and early 1970s, with its heavy investment of financial and emotional capital, now seems to have been over-enthusiastic and ill-judged. Newly built colleges of education have been closed almost as the builders moved out. Universities and polytechnics struggle to maintain their numbers while the newly created Institutes of Higher Education add to the competition. Already, Fresh Horizons students have benefited from the liberalization of entry requirements that has followed. Schools have empty classrooms and sites are cleared as mergers and reorganizations absorb the departing children. There are libraries, pianos, pottery kilns, laboratories, unused. There are teachers and lecturers, specialists of all kinds, redundant and facing redundancy that they never contemplated.

Yet the minuscule resources directly available for adult education are once more being diminished to provide illusory budget savings too small to be reflected in rate or tax levels and the whole enterprise subsists in meagre quarters with sparse equipment grudgingly provided.

A new deal

How much the secondary and tertiary sectors' redundancies can be adapted to serve the quaternary needs of adults needs to be thrashed out in a 'new deal' spirit with administrative barriers down and historic distinctions discarded. This is a clear agenda for the National Advisory Council for Adult Education set up in 1977 as a belated and partial response to the Russell Committee's recommendations. It is not merely a question of making higher education available, with less onerous entry and attendance requirements although this is important and until proper adjustments are made, a large pool of potential ability will remain untapped. Nor can needs for adult education be defined only by reference to the outstandingly disadvantaged and deprived, the rejectors and the rejected, as is the current mode. Their needs are patent enough, but the response too easily smacks of the soup kitchen[21] and the construction of an alibi for failure to face up to the true scale and character of need.

The quaternary phase of education has at one and the same time to serve the lorry driver learning to read, the business man coming to terms with a worker co-director, a saleswoman seeking a sandwich course in management, a graduate mother reading for a higher degree while she raises her family or a motor mechanic who wants a course in jewellery making. The catalogue can be extended endlessly and the same individual may appear many times as the focus of interest and attention changes and another fresh horizon is glimpsed. With some easing of pressure on educational resources, as the high tide of children to be initiated into society recedes, there is a perhaps unique opportunity to reconceive our educational priorities and in doing so to accord later learning the importance and dignity that properly attaches to it.

Postscript

During the time it has taken to prepare this book two of its main themes have come into the forefront of educational consciousness, namely, the need for greatly enlarged access to higher education for mature men and women, and the importance of advisory and counselling services for adults at all levels of educational need.

The first Fresh Horizons students found access to higher education fraught with difficulties, with mature entry to teacher training the most obvious possibility. In the decade since then, the number of university places has increased by more than half. The polytechnics, more locally accessible in London and some major cities, have diversified their offerings from the almost purely technological into arts, business and social studies. The recent opening of a new range of degree courses, in formerly mono-technic colleges of education, has added to the scale and variety of opportunities. These facts, together with the accumulating evidence of achievement by Fresh Horizons students admitted to degree level courses, have eased the paths of later applicants.

The sudden changes in demographic patterns which have occurred in very recent years are reviewed in *Higher Education into the 1990s*, issued as a discussion document by the Department of Education in February 1978. With a pending reduction in the number of potential university entrants at the normal school-leaving age, even government ministers can now sometimes be heard urging the claims of mature students to any vacancies that may arise. Given the age structure among teachers in higher education revealed by that document, such claims may find interested supporters.

We are indebted to Phoebe Lambert, the present Tutor-Organizer, for information about recent Fresh Horizons courses at the City Lit, which reflect these and other changes. Almost all the students on full-time and half of those on part-time courses have, since 1975, been accepted for degree level courses and most of them have been admitted by special arrangements as 'unqualified' entrants.

Some of the changes in the Fresh Horizons courses themselves have been noted in passing. Additionally, since 1976, the two day-time and one evening part-time courses have been extended to thirty weeks. Mathematics has become an optional subject (chosen by one-third of the students), with history as an alternative option.

More Fresh Start courses have emerged elsewhere, two of them with built-in basic science elements. The Nelson and Colne Open College, mentioned on page 177, now has links with some half-dozen other institutions within the region which run similar courses, so that it is now claimed to be possible to speak of an Open College Federation of North-West England. Institutions of higher education have increasingly come to accept Fresh Start courses as recognized channels for mature entry to degree courses. The Nelson and Colne Open College was developed, in the first place, in co-operation with Lancaster University and Preston Polytechnic, and is administered by a committee which reports to the Senate and Academic Boards, respectively, of those institutions. At least one other degree-awarding college is adding a rider to proposed entry requirements that will cover the eligibility of mature applicants if they have satisfactorily completed an approved Fresh Start course.

These developments represent a useful and helpful recognition of the qualities revealed by mature students coming from an experience of study related to their adult capacities and not as specified by examination boards for school-leavers. This is all the more important since we are promised—or threatened with—new 'N' and 'F' levels in the GCE range, by the mid-1980s, and these could again disadvantage the school-leavers of an earlier date.

Special accreditation of preparatory courses for mature students could, however, bring its own hazards. Higher education institutions are properly concerned to maintain standards of entry appropriate to their own needs and may be tempted to try and force Fresh Start courses into a straitjacket of conformity, discouraging the promoters from that continuous exploration and experiment needed to develop individual potentiality in relation to a whole range of possible outcomes.

This widening of possibilities for mature students, as yet hardly more than tentative, makes easily accessible information and counselling services all the more necessary. Adults seeking information and help still, all too often, encounter set-backs such as are indicated in this book, and the greater part of the adult population still does not know that it is possible to make an enquiry at all. Since the publication of the Venables Report in 1976, more has certainly been heard about the need for information, guidance, and counselling, and efforts have been made to give substance to the recommendations that the Open University, through its regional services, should stimulate and support a National Advisory Service for adults.

In this context, it is perhaps not so commonly realized that the National Institute of Adult Education has, for more than a quarter of a century, responded to enquirers, country-wide. Its experience suggests that difficulties arise, not so much in identifying appropriate courses and giving advice that on occasion certainly amounts to counselling, as in being able to point with assurance to a locally available, knowledgeable and helpful person and place able to offer continuing support in exploring whatever possibilities might be indicated.

We feel strongly that financial help for the development of such services would best be channelled to local adult education centres in areas where people live and work, which already have established connections with many agencies of community life and sources of information. The need for such developments has become critical with the growing threat of structural unemployment on a frightening scale. Only a general service of adult education, with adequate resources, can help people not only to seek new identities through work, important as that is, but also to find new potentialities within themselves, to achieve positive satisfactions in new conditions of enforced leisure.

Notes and References

Introduction

1 Enid Hutchinson, 'College of the Air', *Guardian*, 8 February 1963. See also: Enid Hutchinson, 'Crowther and the girls—the dual role', *Education*, vol. 115, May 1960, p. 1140.

2 Enid Hutchinson, 'Second chance', *Education*, vol. 125, January 1965, p. 147.

Chapter 1   Fresh Horizons

1 The now formally adopted name of the City Literary Institute.

2 Two factors—educationally quite irrelevant—contributed to their presence: the fees then charged by the ILEA, which diminished rapidly as a reward for joining more than one class and thus encouraged multiple enrolments; and the fact that transport into central London was relatively cheap but time-consuming. Hence those such as housewives, who made the journey for a class they specially wanted, were tempted to stay and make a day of it. (Prof. H. A. Jones, then Principal, in a private communication.)

3 GCE—abbreviation for General Certificate of Education awarded on the basis of examinations taken in schools in England and Wales at Ordinary—'O'—level by pupils about the age of 16 and at Advanced level—'A'—about the age of 18. GCE certificates are the recognized entry qualifications to sub-professional and professional training. Three 'O's and two 'A's are the normal matriculation requirements for entry to degree-level work. The examinations may be taken in a wide range of academic and some practical subjects. The certificates may be acquired piecemeal at both levels and in this way adults can acquire qualifications gradually in their spare time.

4 See Enid Hutchinson, 'Second Chance', *Education*, vol. 125, January 1965, p. 147.
5 In 1976 courses of thirty weeks were introduced.
6 The introduction of the full-time course in 1973 has not reduced demand for part-time courses. In the three years 1974–5 to 1976–7 enrolments were:

	part-time day	part-time evening†		
	*	W	M	Total
1974–5	36	17	13	30
1975–6	40	16	14	30
1976–7	40	14	12	26
	116	47	39	86

*Almost entirely women.
The percentages recorded as having completed the courses satisfactorily in 1974–5 and 1975–6 were Day—79 per cent; Evening—68 per cent.
†The increased number and proportion of men on evening courses probably reflects a changing economic climate. (Information supplied by Phoebe Lambert, Tutor-Organizer, Fresh Horizons courses, 1977.)

Chapter 2   Winds of change

1 Enid Hutchinson, 'Go spin you jade' (review), *Universities Quarterly*, vol. 12, 1958, pp. 332–6. Enid Hutchinson, 'Women and work', *Adult Education*, vol. 33, 1960, pp. 140–1. Carol Elwood, 'Second chance for women', *Adult Education*, vol. 41, 1968, pp. 221–4. Report—*Opportunities for Women through Education Workshop*.Centre for continuing education of women, University of Michigan, 1965. Helen S. Austin (ed.), *Some Action of Her Own*, Lexington Books, USA, 1976, pp. 1–21. (Recounts the history of continuing education for women in the USA.)
2 Central Statistical Office, 'Social commentary—men and women', *Social Trends*, no. 5, HMSO, London, 1974, p. 12. (Further statistics in this chapter, unless otherwise stated, are from the same source, pp. 1–12.)
3 David Pearce and Malcolm Britton, 'The decline in births—some socio-economic aspects', *Population Trends*, no. 7, HMSO, London, 1977, p. 9. 'Annual births in England and Wales have declined from 784,000 in 1970 to around 585,000 in 1976, a drop of 25 per cent in six years.'
4 Geoffrey Hawthorn, 'The birth-rate and what lies behind it', *New Society*, London, vol. 29, no. 613, p. 11.

5 Editorial, 'Marriage and divorce', *Population Trends*, no. 2, HMSO, London, 1975, p. 1.
6 *Household Spending*, IPC Sociological Monographs, no. 4, IPC, London, 1975, p. 46.
7 Research Department, *The New Housewife, 1973 v 1965*, J. Walter Thompson Co., London, 1975.
8 Penelope Labovitch and Rosemary Simon, *Late Start—careers for wives*, Cornmarket, London, 1966.
9 Beatrice Musgrave and Joan Wheeler Bennett, *Comeback*, Peter Owen, London, 1964.
10 Percentage of school-leavers with 'A' level passes in 1963 and 1973:

	1963		1973	
	Boys	Girls	Boys	Girls
1 or more passes	10·9	7·5	16·5	14·8
2 or more passes	9·0	5·5	13·2	11·3
3 or more passes	6·4	3·1	8·9	6·9

(*Statistics of Education*, vol. 2, *School Leavers, CSE and GCE*, 1973, HMSO, London, 1975).
11 *Statistics of Education*, vol. 3, *Further Education, 1972*, HMSO, London, Table 5.
12 Central Statistical Office, *Social Trends*, no. 5 (op. cit).
13 Russell Committee, *Adult Education—a plan for development*, HMSO, London, 1973, paragraph 26, p. 8.

Chapter 4   Evening students and some comparisons

1 Naomi E. McIntosh with Judith Calder and Betty Swift, *A Degree of Difference*, Society for Research into Higher Education, Ltd, University of Surrey, Guildford, 1976, p. 59.
2 Ibid., p. 115.
3 Ibid., p. 120.

Chapter 5   A full-time course

1 CSE—Certificate of Secondary Education, introduced in 1965. A leaving certificate in school subjects taken by 15- to 16-year-olds. More flexibly devised than GCE 'O' level and intended to test at a lower academic level: only at the top grade is a pass regarded as of equal rating academically.

Chapter 6   Contents of a package

1 'Perhaps the most distinguished of all tutors was T. S. Eliot who conducted his literature class at Southall over three sessions 1916–18 (course fee: 2s.). When he first offered his services to BPEUT his subjects, eleven in all, embraced not only various aspects of literature but

also (10) sociology of primitive peoples and (11) social psychology. Although his application to give tutorial classes was approved there was apparently some doubt about adding his name to the supplementary list of university extension lecturers'—John Burrows, *University Adult Education in London—a century of achievement*, University of London, 1976, p. 43.

2 I. A. Richards, *Interpretation in Teaching*, Routledge & Kegan Paul, London, 1938 (reissued 1973), p. 4.

Chapter 7 The counselling element

1 Jonathan F. Brown and Eileen M. Aird, *New Opportunities Courses at Newcastle*, Department of Adult Education, University of Newcastle-upon-Tyne, p. 7.

2 Patricia Thom, Anne Ironside and Eileen Hendry, 'The Women's Resources Centre', *Adult Leadership*, 1975, pp. 129–32.

3 Peter Hewitt, *After School English*, National Extension College, Shaftesbury Road, Cambridge, 1967.

Chapter 9 Those who got away

1 These were particularly disruptive of the lives of the commuters and housewives, especially those with children at school. They included: transport stoppages, 1967; February–April 1973; January–February 1974. Selective and other stoppages by teachers in schools, November 1969–March 1970 and February 1973. Industrial action by electricity workers, December 1970–March 1971 and November–December 1973. A strike in the gas industry, December 1972–March 1973, led to the closure of educational establishments, including the City Lit: the introduction of the three-day week, December 1973 extended into the early part of the following year.

Chapter 10 A counselling service in adult education

1 Enid Hutchinson, 'Counselling—needs to be met', *Adult Education*, vol. 42, 1969, pp. 29–38.

2 Naomi McIntosh, *et al.*, *A Degree of Difference*, Society for Research into Higher Education, Ltd, University of Surrey, Guildford, 1976, p. 89.

3 Stuart Maclure, *Access to Continuing Education*, Conference Report, ed. Paul Fordham, Open University, Milton Keynes, 1976, p. 65.

4 Russell Committee, *Adult Education—a plan for development*, HMSO, London, 1973, paragraph 189, p. 190.

5 Audrey Newsome, Bryan J. Thorne and Keith L. Wyld, *Student Counselling in Practice*, University of London Press, 1973, p. 10.

6 Donald H. Blocher, *Developmental Counselling*, Ronald Press, New York, 1966, p. 65.
7 Trefor Vaughan, *Education and the Aims of Counselling*, Basil Blackwell, Oxford, 1973, p. 43.
8 H. Jackson, *Some Aspects of Counselling and Guidance at the Higher Education Level*, UNESCO, Paris, 1973, p. 39.
9 Newsome, Thorne and Wyld, op. cit., pp. 7–8.
10 Vaughan, op. cit., p. 3.

Chapter 11   In residence—an earlier model

1 Russell Committee, *Adult Education—a plan for development*, HMSO, London, 1973, paragraph 253, p. 85.

Chapter 12   Alternative routes

1 Russell Committee, *Adult Education—a plan for development*, HMSO, London, 1973, paragraph 1.3, p. 18.
2 Jim Ingram, *The World's My University*, Harrap, London, 1965.
3 Russell Committee, op. cit., paragraph 247, p. 83.
4 Ibid., paragraph 46.1, p. 14.
5 Ibid., paragraph 47, p. 15.
6 Ibid., paragraph 58.1.3, p. 18.
7 Ibid., paragraph 145, p. 47.
8 Ibid., paragraph 289, p. 97.
9 Committee on Continuing Education, *Interim Report*, Open University, Milton Keynes, 1976, p. 23.
10 Ibid., p. 23.
11 Committee on Continuing Education, *Final Report*, Open University, Milton Keynes, 1976, p. 53.
12 Russell Committee, op. cit., paragraph 145, p. 47.
13 Ruth Michaels, *New Opportunities for Women*, Hatfield Polytechnic, Hatfield, Herts, 1973.
14 Jonathan F. Brown, 'What shall we do with new opportunities courses?', *Adult Education*, vol. 49, 1976, pp. 42–4.
15 Committee on Continuing Education, *Interim Report*, op. cit., p. 25.
16 The Russell Committee noted, in relation to the difficulties of students at long-term residential colleges, at that time eligible only for discretionary grants:

> An obvious solution is to make any one selected for a long-term residential course automatically eligible for a mandatory award.
> However we appreciate that this would require legislation and, as it would involve a whole range of other one- and two-year courses might at present prove unacceptable.
>
> (op. cit., paragraph 303, p. 100).

Nevertheless, special provision was made specifically for students at the residential colleges in the Education Act, 1975, Section 2 and these, whether they are actually resident or not, can and do receive mandatory grants via their local education authorities. Since authorities' policies regarding the making of discretionary grants vary considerably, and since such provision is susceptible to attack when cuts in public spending are imposed, applicants for full-time non-residential courses elsewhere are clearly discriminated against in this matter. Part-time students also find arbitrary increases in fees, imposed at short notice, an embarrassment amounting to a deterrent at such times.

17 Russell Committee, op. cit., paragraph 257, p. 87.
18 Naomi McIntosh *et al.*, *A Degree of Difference*, Society for Research into Higher Education, Ltd, University of Surrey, Guildford, 1976, p. i (preface).
19 David Pearce and Malcolm Britton, 'The decline in births—some socio-economic aspects', *Population Trends*, no. 7, HMSO, London, 1977, p. 9.
20 James Joyce, *Ulysses*, Penguin, Harmondsworth, 1969, p. 607.
21 Brian Groombridge, *Adult Education and the Multi-Media Systems*, Conference Report, European Bureau of Adult Education, Amersfoort, PO Box 367, Netherlands, p. 67.

Index